George F. Mulvany, Henry E. Doyle

Catalogue, descriptive and historical, of the works of art in the National Gallery of Ireland

With short biographical, descriptive and critical notes

George F. Mulvany, Henry E. Doyle

Catalogue, descriptive and historical, of the works of art in the National Gallery of Ireland
With short biographical, descriptive and critical notes

ISBN/EAN: 9783742897459

Manufactured in Europe, USA, Canada, Australia, Japa

Cover: Foto ©Andreas Hilbeck / pixelio.de

Manufactured and distributed by brebook publishing software
(www.brebook.com)

George F. Mulvany, Henry E. Doyle

Catalogue, descriptive and historical, of the works of art in the National Gallery of Ireland

ARS EMOLLIT MORES.

CATALOGUE,

DESCRIPTIVE AND HISTORICA

OF THE

WORKS OF ART

IN THE

NATIONAL GALLERY OF IR

WITH

SHORT BIOGRAPHICAL, DESCRIPTIV CRITICAL NOTES.

COMPILED BY THE LATE

GEORGE F. MULVANY, R.H.A.,

(FIRST DIRECTOR OF THE GALLERY).

CONTINUED AND REVISED BY

HENRY E. DOYLE, C.B., R.H.A.,

DIRECTOR.

By Authority.

DUBLIN:

PRINTED BY ALEX. THOM & CO., 87, 88, & 89, ABBEY-ST.,

THE QUEEN'S PRINTING OFFICE.

FOR HER MAJESTY'S STATIONERY OFFICE.

1882.

NATIONAL GALLERY OF IRELAND.

Board of Governors and Guardians.

CONTENTS

PREFATORY NOTICE.

THE interest excited by the collection of Paintings brought together at the great Exhibition in Dublin, in 1853, suggested the feasibility of establishing a National Gallery, which had been long desired by all lovers of Art, and deemed essential to the advancement of Art in Ireland. At the close of that Exhibition a number of noblemen and gentlemen united to form an association designated " The Irish Institution," for the purpose of holding annual Exhibitions of contributed works, with the ultimate view of establishing a permanent Gallery. It held its first Exhibition at the Royal Hibernian Academy, in 1854, and continued its annual Exhibitions for several years.

The Committee of the Dargan Testimonial Fund, in the year 1854, determined to vote a sum of £5,000 out of the funds contributed to commemorate the public services of William Dargan, Esq., as the Founder of the Exhibition of 1853, towards the erection of a Public Gallery of Art ; and aided by Act of Parliament, with the concurrence of the Royal Dublin Society, a site having been obtained on Leinster Lawn for the National Gallery of Ireland, the necessary additional funds were contributed, from time to time, by Parliamentary Grants, to the amount of £21,500.

By Acts 17 and 18 Vic., cap. 99 (1854), and 18 and 19 Vic., cap. 44 (1855), a Board of Governors and Guardians was incorporated. It consists of seventeen members, of whom five are *ex officio*—namely, the President (the Lord Lieutenant for the time being) and the senior Vice-President of the Royal Dublin Society, the President of the Royal Hibernian Academy, the President of the Royal Irish Academy, and the

Chairman of the Board of Works. Of the remaining twelve, two are to be Artists resident in Ireland, delegated by the Royal Hibernian Academy; three are appointed by Government; and seven are to be elected, from time to time, as vacancies occur, by a constituency of all Annual Subscribers of One Guinea or upwards, all Donors of £10 or upwards as Life Members, and all Donors of Works of Art accepted by the Board and by them valued at £20 or upwards. These twelve Governors hold office for five years only; but are eligible for re-election.

The collection of Paintings now brought together consists of works purchased by means of private subscriptions, aided by an annual Parliamentary Grant, of works presented or bequeathed, and others deposited by the Trustees of the National Gallery of England.

The Casts after the Antique and other works of Sculpture have been obtained, by a Treasury Order for a portion, from the British Museum, aided by the funds of the Ancient Art Society, and by private donations and subscriptions.

THE NATIONAL GALLERY OF IRELAND is open to the Public, subject to the regulations of the Board, on MONDAYS, TUESDAYS, WEDNESDAYS, and THURSDAYS from NOON to DUSK (or 6 o'clock, P.M.), and on SUNDAYS from 2 P.M. to 5 P.M., or DUSK; admission free. Reserved for Artists and Students on FRIDAYS and SATURDAYS from 10 A.M. to 4 P.M.; admission to the Public Six Pence. SUBSCRIBERS and DONORS to the Gallery, entitled to vote at Elections for Members of the Board, are admitted on reserved days, free. On such evenings, during periods as are fixed by the Board, and notified by advertisement, the GALLERY, LIGHTED BY GAS, will be open from 8 to 10 o'clock. Admission, free.

DONATIONS

FOR THE

PURCHASE OF WORKS OF ART FOR THE NATIONAL GALLERY OF IRELAND.

It is important to state that the Lords Commissioners of Her Majesty's Treasury have expressed their readiness to sanction grants of public money for the purchase of Works of Art equivalent to private donations, and to permit the money value of any Work of Art presented, as appraised by the Governors, to count as a pecuniary donation.

(The names of Donors of Works of Art are in all cases affixed to the works themselves).

Donations received to the 31st January, 1864, when the Gallery was opened to the public.

DONATION FUND.

	£	s.		£	s.
Her Majesty the Queen,	100	0	The Viscount Massereene and		
H.R.H. The Prince Consort (the			Ferrard (the late),	10	0
late),	50	0	The Viscount Palmerston,M.P.		
H.R.H. The Prince of Wales,	50	0	(the late), by eight annual pay		
The Earl of Carlisle (the late),			ments, £8 8s. (and £21 donation),	29	8
when Lord Lieutenant,	100	0	The Viscount Powerscourt,	10	0
The Earl of Eglinton (the late),			The Viscount Southwell (the late),	5	0
when Lord Lieutenant of Ireland,	100	0	The Bishop of Derry, &c.(the late),	10	0
The Lord Primate of Ireland,	10	0	The Bishop of Limerick, &c. (the		
The Lord Primate of Ireland (the			late),	10	0
late),	100	0	The Lord Annaly,	5	0
The Right Hon. Francis Blackburne, Lord Chancellor, when			The Lord Carbery,	15	0
			The Lord Castlemaine (the late),	5	0
Lord Justice of Appeal (the			The Lord Clarina,	5	0
late),	10	0	The Lord Clermont,	10	0
The Right Hon. Sir Maziere			The Lord Cloncurry (the late),	10	0
Brady, Bart., when Lord Chancellor of Ireland,	1,250	0	The Lord De Freyne (the late),	10	0
			The Lord Digby,	10	0
The Duke of Devonshire (the late),	50	0	The Lord Herbert of Lea (the late),	10	0
The Duke of Leinster,	50	0	The Lord Inchiquin,	10	0
The Marquis of Kildare,	10	0	The Lord Rossmore (the late),	5	0
The Marquis of Lansdowne (the			The Lord Talbot de Malahide,	10	10
late),	10	0	The Right Hon. Baron Greene		
The Marquis of Londonderry, by			(the late),	10	0
nine annual payments,	90	0	The Right Hon. W. F. F. Tighe,	10	0
The Marquis of Waterford (the			Sir Chas. H. Coote, Bart., D.L. by		
late),	20	0	annual payments (the late),	50	0
The Earl Annesley,	10	0	Sir Compton Domvile, Bart. (the		
The Earl of Bective,	5	0	late),	10	0
The Earl of Belmore,	5	0	Sir Richard J. Griffith, Bart.,LL.D.	25	0
The Earl of Charlemont (the late),	20	0	Sir George F. J. Hodson, Bart.,		
The Earl Dudley,	5	0	D.L.,	5	5
The Earl of Egmont,	10	0	Sir Bernard Burke,	5	0
The Earl of Enniskillen,	5	0	Stewart Blacker, Esq., J.P.,	10	10
The Earl Fitzwilliam (the late),	10	0	William Brocas, Esq., R.H.A. (the		
The Earl of Lanesborough (the late),	10	0	late),	10	0
The Earl of Meath,	10	0	William Brooke, Esq., M.C.	5	0
The Earl of Ranfurly (the late),	5	0	Colonel Maxwell Close, D.L. (the		
The Earl of Roden,	10	0	late),	5	0
The Earl of Wicklow (the late),	10	0	Anthony Cliffe, Esq., D.L.	3	0
The Viscount Bangor,	5	0	Edward J. Cooper, Esq., F.R.S. (the late),	10	0

	£	s.		£	s.
M. Corr Vander Maeren (Brussels),	5	0	John C. Lyons, Esq.	5	0
Gallery of Ancient Art,	248	6	William Malone, Esq..	1	1
Ven. Archdeacon of Glandelough			Edward Nolan, Esq.	5	0
(the late),	3	3	William Smith O'Brien, Esq. (the		
Sir Benjamin L. Guinness, Bart.,			late), first donation,	2	0
LL.D. (the late),	100	0	Jonathan Pim, Esq., M.P.,	10	0
John Hamilton, Esq., M.D.	3	0	William Harvey Pim, Esq.,	10	0
Henry Kemmis, Esq., Q.C. (the			John G. V. Porter, Esq., D.L.,	10	0
late),	10	0	John Radcliff, Esq. (the late),	5	0
Major-General Sir T. A. Larcom,			Royal Irish Art-Union,	240	0
Bart., K.C.B.	10	10	Lieut.-Colonel W. B. R. Smith,	2	0
N. P. Leader, Esq., J.P., M.P.,			Edward Tighe, Esq. (the late),	10	0
Dromagh Castle,	25	0	George Woods, Esq., J.P.,	10	10
James W. J. Lendrick, Esq., Q.C.	3	0			

RECEIVED SINCE:

	£	s.		£	s.
Wm. Dargan, Esq. (the late),	2,000	0	Mrs. Grattan (the late)	5	0
Wm. Justin O'Driscoll, Esq.	10	0	Henry Bussell, Esq.,	1	1
T. Maxwell Hutton, Esq.,	2	2	Gallery of Ancient Art(balance),	29	0
Mrs. T. M. Hutton,	1	1	Right Hon. Sir J. Napier, Bart.,	5	0
John Stevenson, Esq.,	1	1	Right Hon. Sir Maziere Brady,		
Alex. Thom, Esq.,	10	0	Bart., second donation,	700	0
Duke of Leinster,	1	1	The Marquis of Londonderry, by		
Wm. Smith O'Brien (the late),			three annual payments,	30	0
second donation,	2	0	John Ribton Garstin, F.S.A.,	10	0
Sir Robert L. Blosse, Bart..	5	0	Dr. Barry,	100	0
E. H. Scriven, Esq., M.D.,	1	1			

Donations may be lodged in the Bank of Ireland, or any of its local branches, to the credit of the Treasurer, (Lord Talbot de Malahide); or remitted to

HENRY E. DOYLE,

Director.

NATIONAL GALLERY OF IRELAND,
MERRION-SQUARE, WEST, DUBLIN.

INTRODUCTION.

ANCIENT MASTERS.

THE important facts of the History of Painting may be condensed within a short space. From the earliest date, some knowledge and practice of design and use of colours can be traced. The drawing, indeed, at first, like that of children, was conventional or representative rather than imitative; the colour uniform, sometimes flat or opaque; but totally devoid of any treatment in light or shade. Such are the paintings in the ruins of Nineveh, Egypt, Etruria; more or less advanced, but still merely symbolical or representative. The nice appreciation of form—the distinctions between generic characteristics and accidental details—beauty—expression—chiaro-scuro, and perspective—are the results of highly advanced civilization; and centuries elapse in the process of development.

In Greece, sculpture had been brought to great perfection, while painting was in a minor or ornamental phase. The brother of the great sculptor, Phidias, was, according to some authorities, merely a decorative artist; others assert that he aided Phidias with historical paintings in the decoration of his temples. Pausanius describes Polignotus as decorating the walls of temples and other buildings in a style grand but dry; hard and careful. Pliny describes Parrhasius, of Ephesus, as the first painter who gave symmetry to his figures, about four hundred years before Christ. Zeuxis was distinguished by daring truth of character and idealization. About seventy years after him, Apelles is said to have brought colouring to perfection, and to have astonished men by the expression of human emotions, and a grace and loveliness, as in the Venus Anadyomene, which inspired the verse of Anacreon. No vestiges of these works remain, so that we must take their excellence on the authority of contemporary or subsequent writers. It is only fair to assume that a nation which arrived at great perfection in sculpture and architecture could not have failed to cultivate painting with success.

It is important to remark how the development of the imitative arts was simultaneous with that of science and literature. In fact, the plastic arts gave visible form to the successive degrees of knowledge which the philosophers attained in the study of man and nature. Socrates and Phidias, Sophocles and Polignotus were contemporaries.

From the Grecian epoch of art, in which painting rose to its highest point of excellence under Apelles, about 368 years before Christ, no artist of note appeared—at least no marked development is recorded—until the thirteenth century of the Christian era. Painting was, nevertheless, continuously practised. When the Romans conquered Greece, they not only despoiled the temples and forums of their art decorations, but they brought Greek artists into Italy, whose skill was made to subserve the luxury rather than the taste of their conquerors. When Constantinople became the seat of empire, these Grecian artists followed in the train of their conquerors; and thus the school of art known as the Byzantine grew up. In this school, something of the early Christian art of Rome, Asiatic symbolism, and the technical traditions of Greek art, were combined; conventionalism prevailed over truth of imitation or iconic force. During the tenth and eleventh centuries the Byzantine practice prevailed through Italy and Northern Europe, and its influence obtained to an advanced period in the Italian and German schools.

In Tuscany, in the thirteenth century, under Cimabue and his pupil, Giotto, art received a new impulse, a more spiritual direction. Nearly three centuries elapsed from their time to the culmination of art under Leonardo da Vinci, Michel Angelo, and Raphael, about 1500–30.

The earliest modes of painting were in tempera and fresco. In the former the colours were mixed with gluten or size, as in modern "body colours," and the pictures were ultimately varnished. In fresco the colours are mixed with water and laid upon fresh plaster. This method requires great mastery and certainty of execution, besides the careful preliminary preparation of tinted drawings the full size of the work, termed cartoons. To John Van Eyck, of Bruges, is attributed the discovery of oil painting in 1410. Previous to the time of the Van Eycks, oil painting had been in common use for walls, wood-work, and statuary, exposed to the open air; but pictures even on panels were painted in tempera and subsequently varnished. It is said that the oil varnish in use required exposure to the sun's heat to expedite its drying, and thus that Van Eyck had a fine picture destroyed by the splitting of the panel. This was just as likely to occur in first painting with oil; and most probably the Van Eycks' efforts were directed to the discovery of a good drying oil, or they incorporated an improved varnish with the linseed oil in ordinary use.* The monk, Theophilus, has described the oils and varnishes in use in housepainting and such ordinary use so early as the eleventh century. Whatever be the claims of the Brothers Van Eyck to the first use of oil in easel or other pictures, it is quite certain that they introduced the best, most brilliant, and permanent manner of painting in oil, and that from their invention arose its general use.

* See Merimée on the art of painting in oil and fresco.

SCHOOLS OF PAINTING.

The distinction of schools is somewhat arbitrary, even when in the broadest sense they include the painters of an entire country; the description of their characteristics is even more so, especially when the minor schools of particular cities or districts, or the followers of any particular master are concerned. It is only intended to point out here the leading schools of Europe, the principal artists of these, and the salient distinctions of aim and development. Every spectator will be more or less influenced in his estimate of various works by the peculiar bent of his own mind, and be pleased in proportion as his sympathies are enlisted in the subject, or his particular taste is satisfied by the performance. It is ever to be borne in mind as to the earlier masters, that they can be only justly appreciated having reference to the period at which they painted, the comparative excellence or inferiority of their predecessors, and the intention of their works in harmony with the spirit and the requirement of their age.

The Italian schools are usually divided into four, viz. :—the FLORENTINE, ROMAN, VENETIAN, and LOMBARD ; all the minor schools, such as those of Umbria, Parma, Ferrara, Cremona, Siénna, Milan, may be regarded as subdivisions of the four principal ; the Neapolitan showed an admixture, in a great degree, of Italian and Spanish influences.

THE FLORENTINE or TUSCAN SCHOOL dates from an early period of the thirteenth century, commencing with Cimabue, assuming still more remarkable development with Giotto. Among the most distinguished artists of this school during the fourteenth and fifteenth centuries were Taddeo Gaddi, Fra Angelico, Paolo Uccello, Masaccio, Fra Filippo Lippi, Pesellino, Benozzo Gozzoli, Ghirlandajo, Roselli, Sandro Boticelli, and Lorenzo Credi. It reached its highest point of excellence in the sixteenth century under Leonardo Da Vinci and Michel Angelo. It may be observed of those Florentine artists, from Cimabue and Giotto to Da Vinci and Michel Angelo, that they were characterized by greatness of aim or motive ; by severity of design, and intensity of expression. By the earliest artists individual form was closely imitated ; while Michel Angelo aimed at sublimity through abstract or ideal form and generic character, which sometimes seems overcharged and extravagant. In his works we look for grandeur, dignity, and power, rather than for grace or beauty. Out of Italy he is chiefly known through the copyist or engraver ; as he is said to have despised oil painting as "an art only fit for women." His designs have, however, been handed down in oil by Pontormo, Bronzino, Marcello Venusti, and others ; he evidently aided Sebastian del Piombo in his great work, the raising of Lazarus. He does not seem to have founded in any extended sense, a school. On the other hand, Da Vinci, who studied nature with a philosophic appreciation, gave expression to the emotions and passions, and cultivated a refined truth and richness of imitation, had a more

extended influence on his cotemporaries and followers. His Last
Supper, painted for the refectory of the convent St. Maria-delle
Grazie, at Milan, was his greatest work.   Of his immediate school,
Cesare da Sesto, by whom a work of great perfection is in this
collection, was esteemed the best; Luini sedulously copied his
manner, as did also Beltraffio, Melzi, and others.

THE ROMAN SCHOOL would seem more properly a branch of the
Florentine, for Raphael, who was its leader, had worked and
studied long in Florence, and had much in common with Leonardo
and Michel Angelo as to high invention and design; though he
cultivated ideal beauty more, and individual or generic character
less, than either of his great contemporaries.   The chief works
of this great triumvirate are in fresco in Milan, in Florence, and
in Rome; easel works in oil, by Da Vinci and Raphael, are found
in public and private galleries.   In Raphael's time the discovery of
many remains of ancient sculpture gave a new direction to art
development.   From their study he improved his sense of ideal
beauty; adopted more freedom of truth and design, justness of
expression, and more flowing and graceful treatment of drapery,
than belonged to his early style, formed on that of his master,
Perugino.   Giulio Romano, Polidoro Caldara, Piero del Vaga,
Andrea Sabattini, called da Salerno, and Giovani Udine, are the
most distinguished of Raphael's pupils; of his imitators, who
were numerous, the chief were Andrea del Sarto and Sassoferratto.
We have seen that the course of the Tuscan or Florentine School
was one of progress and ascension from the thirteenth to the sixteenth century, terminating then as a distinct school; the Roman
School first taking position in the sixteenth century, with Raphael
as its head, declined thenceforth, albeit so many artists of great
excellence belonged to it.

THE VENETIAN SCHOOL, though dating from the thirteenth century, owes its real development to the Bellini, in the fifteenth
century, more especially to Giovanni, who, it is said, first appre-
hended the true scope and power of painting in oil, as it was
introduced by Antonello da Messina, who is recorded to have
visited the Van Eycks, and having acquired the knowledge of oil
painting in their school to have imported it into Italy.   Carlo
Crivelli, Vivarini, Basaita, and Giambatista Cima, belong properly
to that century; though exhibiting great beauty of colour and
detail, partaking still of conventional stiffness.   In the sixteenth
century Giorgione, Titian, Pordenone, Sebastiano del Piombo,
Bartolommeo Veneziano, Il Moretti, G. B. Moroni, Paris Bordone,
Ghirlandajo da Treviso, Jacopo Bassano, Tintoretto, and Paolo
Veronese, formed a constellation, for vigour, power, and variety unsurpassed in any other school.   If in the Florentine and Roman
Schools form, expression, and ideal beauty were marvellously cul
tivated, in the Venetian the full force of colour, as it aided in life-
like representation, in enhancing the charm of form, in aiding, as
Kugler says, " in the expression of characteristic and elevated
conception," was first fully exhibited.   "It is," he says again, "the

enjoyment of life and all its splendour which speaks in the noble production of their school." If the Flemings invented or brought oil painting to perfection, the Venetian artists may be said to have used it to exhibit, by the aid of harmony and brilliancy of colour, the noblest conceptions of human life, of art, and nature. In portraiture they have never been surpassed. The chief faults of the school were sensuality of treatment, indifference to accurate design, anachronism in costume—faults sometimes exhibited even in the works of its great men.

THE LOMBARD SCHOOL embraced at least three subdivisions— the School of Parma, with Correggio as its founder and chief, six-teenth century; that of Cremona, commencing with Francesco and Philippo Tacconi in the fifteenth century, and more known as that of the Campi in the sixteenth century; and that of Milan, commencing in the fifteenth, and distinguished as early as the sixteenth century by Ambrogio, Borgognone, Bramantino, Bel-traffio, Bernardino Lanini, and, towards its close, by Giulio Cesare Procaccini, who, with his brother, Camillo, founded a distinct school. Of all these, Antonio Allegri da Correggio stands foremost and unrivalled. With a true apprehension of life and colour, and the play of form, he aided their fullest expression by a thorough comprehension of the principles of light and shade, perspec-tive and foreshortening, so as to give the truest relief, repose, and space of any previous artist. His very excellence, however, led to extravagance and seeming affectation. Francesco Maria Ron-dani (see catalogue) was one of his few pupils; but he had many imitators, among whom Parmigiano was accounted the best.

The School of Bologna should properly rank as one of the leading Italian schools, for it dates from the fifteenth century, with Francia and Lorenzo Costa; while in the sixteenth and seventeenth, it was distinguished by the Caracci, Domenichino, Guido Reni, Guercino, and P. Francesco Mola. Lanfranco seems to have belonged equally to the Lombard and the Bologna school. The schools of which Annibale Carracci, G. Cesare Procaccini, and the Campi of Cremona, were the chief masters, have been termed Eclectic, because of their devotion to the works of other masters, selecting and seeking to unite in their own works some of their best qualities; but not, however, ex-cluding the study of nature. Opposed to them were the *Natura-listi*, who, as the term implies, based their study on nature alone, or rather upon its individual types—of these, the most remarkable were Caravaggio, Ribera (called Lo Spagnoletto), and Salvator Rosa; the two latter being in fact the founders of the Neapolitan school. Works by most of the artists here referred to, will be found in this collection.

THE GERMAN SCHOOL, of all others in Europe after the Italian, bears most the stamp of distinct generic characters. It origi-nated in the so-called Rhenan-Byzantine period. When the Roman arms expanded by conquest and colonization toward the north of Europe, across the Danube, and along the Rhine, they carried with them the arts, such as they existed amongst them.

Cologne and Nuremberg were the first seats of Germanic art. In the former, towards the close of the fourteenth century, Meister Wilhelm appeared, and awoke a new spirit of art from the cere-clothes of conventionality and mannerism. Kugler says of the works of the School of Cologne: "They are impressed with so pure, and, considering the general progress of art, so complete a feeling for beauty—ideal conception, and truthful imitation of nature, are blended so happily—that we look in vain in the succeeding periods of German art for so high a degree of perfection. A peculiar sweetness of expression and a child-like serenity and grace are shed over these figures." The celebrated picture in the cathedral of Cologne, by Meister Stephan, pupil of Meister Wilhelm, sustains, in most respects, Kugler's eulogistic criticisms.

In the fifteenth and sixteenth centuries a School of Art arose in Westphalia, assuming as its type the motives and manner of the Van Eycks. Albert Durer, born in Nuremburg in 1471, died there in 1528. A style somewhat analogous to that of the School of Cologne had gradually been developed in that city during the fifteenth century. Albert Durer brought it to its highest perfection, and indelibly stamped his name and style on the Nuremberg School.

Contemporaneously, the School of Saxony, with Lucas Cranach at its head, assumed a distinct character.

In the Dutch School the mechanical portion of painting was brought to the highest degree of excellence. In colouring, composition, arrangement of light and shade, and truth of imitation, the Dutch painters have not been surpassed by any other. They eschewed ideal beauty, and copied nature just as they found it; hence, in their best works, much that is mean and commonplace may be found; yet the truth and force of nature invests them with fascination.

With Lucas Van Leyden, who died in 1533, the early fame of Dutch art is linked; but its true development commenced with Mirevelt, Morelze, John Van Ravestyn, and Francis Hals, who all lived and practised between 1566 and 1666. These latter artists painted portrait almost exclusively—a branch of art in which Van der Helst reached great perfection in the same century. Rembrandt belongs to the same period, but stands alone by the originality of his style, the vigour of his pencil, and the magic arrangement of colour and chiaro-scuro; while his pupils, Ferdinand Bol, Eckhout, and P. de Koning, well sustain the reputation of his school.

Teniers, Ostade, Bega, Jan Steen, Brauwer, Jan Molinaer, Gerard Dow, Metzu, and Terburg, are the exponents of a new development of painting in the seventeenth century. *Genre*-painting, as it is called, "comprises," says Kugler, "the representation of common life in its everyday relations, as opposed to religious and heroic subjects;" and we can easily comprehend how completely such a development was suited to the temperament and character of the Hollanders.

Landscape painting, as a distinct branch of art, was first practised in the close of the sixteenth or early in the seventeenth century. Its earliest phase, under Brueghel, Paul Bril, Roland Savery, and others, partook of a conventional treatment. Savery, indeed, infused a deep feeling and more poetic meaning than any one had previously done, into scenes studied faithfully after nature. Everdingen, Ruysdael, Hobbema, Both, Cuyp, Wouwerman, Berghem, Adrian Van den Velde, and many more, cultivated landscape with wonderful success. Some of these treated it as subsidiary to, or deriving interest from, groups of animal; others, like Weenix, in connexion with dead game. De Heem, Van Huysum, and Mignon, painted fruit, flowers, and so-called still-life with wonderful truth and finish.

THE FLEMISH SCHOOL, from the long connexion—the almost geographical unity of Holland and Flanders—is often confounded with the Dutch; yet the motives are as distinct as the characters of the people and their religious tendencies are different.

Two distinct schools, and at distant intervals, arose in Belgium —the first being the old Flemish, of which the brothers John and Hubert Van Eyck were the founders in the fifteenth century; the second, called the School of Brabant, arose with Rubens, in the seventeenth century.

John Van Eyck is the reputed inventor of painting in oil. But the improvements in the aim and power of art which he and Hubert, his elder brother, exhibited in their works, was of far greater importance to the progress of art. Instead of the stiff conventional figures—the gilded back grounds—the traditional legacies of Byzantine art—they gave an earnestness of life and individual character to their heads—rich mellow colouring to their figures, and introduced highly finished landscape back grounds. For luminous effect their works have never been surpassed. The chief of these executed by the two brothers is at Ghent. Their works, as well as those of their most distinguished follower, Hans Memling, retained still something of the rigidity of their prototypes, and the geometrical symmetry of composition.

During the sixteenth century Flemish art may be said to have been in a state of transition. Italy had become the Mecca of art pilgrimage; and such men as Bernard Van Orley, Coxcie, Van Kalker, Mabuse, Pierre Koeck, Van Cleef, and Otto Venius, going to study in the Roman, Venetian, and Lombardic Schools, brought back the ideas and motives of their several developments, to combine them more or less happily with the practice of the Van Eyck School. Quentin Matsys did not visit Italy, yet in some of his works there is a spiritual treatment combined with wonderful elaboration of details.

Rubens came, at the close of the sixteenth century, as the crowning point of its progressive transition, and burst forth in the seventeenth as a very phenomenon of art. Opposing the mannerism which had grown up by reason of the practice of his predecessors, in studying more the works of other artists than striving to evoke new principles, he dared a course for himself, and by the originality of his purpose, founded a second Flemish School, called, more properly, the School of Brabant. Vandyke was his most distinguished pupil.

THE FRENCH SCHOOL was, until at least the seventeenth century, dependent upon foreign genius for its art. From Italy, on the one hand, and Flanders on the other, occasionally the best artists went to practise in France; and her nascent school partook largely of the elements of both her neighbours. It is true, that through the means of illustrated manuscripts, native talent can be traced to a very early date. King René, of Anjou, was painter as well as poet, and is said to have imbibed somewhat of the style of Van Eyck, from a three years' imprisonment at Dijon and Bracon, between 1431 and 1436. Another *enlumineur*, Jean Fouquet, of Tours, is mentioned as court painter of Louis XI. His works are spoken of by Dr. Waagen as well designed.

It is well known that Leonardo da Vinci expired in France; and that, previously, Giotto had painted some frescoes in Avignon, and also in other parts of France.

Jean Cousin, born in 1462, is said to have been the founder of the French School; but though the names and works of several subsequent native artists are known, the first great one is that of Nicholas Poussin, who was born in 1594. His style was formed entirely on the Italian type, and he seems to have venerated the antique as much as Rembrandt is said to have undervalued it. There is little doubt that his works would have been more effective had he conjoined the *naturalism* and luminousness of the Flemish School with Italian classicism. His nephew by marriage, Gaspar Dughet, known as Gaspar Poussin, and his contemporary, Claude Gelée de Lorraine, although both French, are more usually classed with the Italian School. Claude, although he was the pupil of Tassi, who studied under Paul Bril, a Flemish artist, evidently drew his inspirations more from Italian ideas and Italian skies than from those of France; which country has, however, the right to claim him as her son.

Vouet was the jealous rival of Poussin, but time has assured the superiority of the latter artist. Le Sueur and Le Brun were both pupils of Vouet, and have enrolled their names among the notabilities of France. These artists, however, have little to distinguish their school as essentially French—it was rather the reflex of the art of other countries.

Between them and David numerous clever artists are found, the most distinguished being Jouvenet, Rigaud, Watteau, and Vernet. By the instrumentality of Le Brun and the celebrated Colbert, the Royal Academy of Fine Arts had been established in France in the year 1648. David, born a century after, was the founder of a new French School, which had little reality or original force, and only exercised, for some time, an injurious influence on French art. The most distinguished amongst his followers were

Geràrd and Géricault. The first well known by his able picture of the "Entrance of Henry IV. into Paris;" the second, by his "Wreck of the Medusa."

In the Spanish School the development of art exhibited more of a national character than in that of France. The early records of art in Spain are vague; and although Palomino Velasco, in the third volume of his Treatise on Painting, has given the lives of Spanish Artists, and Cean Bermudez, a later and more reliable authority, has published a dictionary of painters, it is believed that the early history of art in Spain has not as yet been fully investigated.

Cean Bermudez mentions the names of illuminators of manuscripts so early as the tenth century; and in the records of the painted chamber of Westminster, a payment is noted to Petrus de Hispania, in the 37th year of Henry III. (1253). From the intimate relations which subsisted between Spain and the Low Countries, it is but natural to infer that the art and artists of Flanders found encouragement and employment from the kings and grandees of Spain. Roger Van der Weyden, commonly called Roger of Bruges, a distinguished scholar of Van Eyck, is supposed to have practised in Spain in the fifteenth century, being known as Maestro Rogel; and John Van Eyck himself was sent into Portugal, by Philip the Good of Burgundy, to paint Isabel, daughter of John I. of Portugal, whose hand Philip sought in marriage. At the same time the German taste and practice was widely diffused in Spain, and native painters are named, such as Gallegos, whose works are said to have approached those of Albert Durer.

In the sixteenth century the influence of Italian art permeated through the schools of Spain. Italian artists were received and practised there; whilst Spanish painters frequented the schools of Italy, returning with refined taste, but still exhibiting the *naturalist* character of Spanish art in their works. The most distinguished of the foreign visitors was Titian,* who was invited and honourably received by Charles V. The native artist who was most celebrated in this period was Luis Morales, called the Divine.

The true development of the national genius for art was in the seventeenth century, and the names of Alonzo Cano, Zurbaran, Velazquez, Murillo. rank in the history of European as well as Spanish art, amongst the most notable; until lately their works have been little known out of Spain, and even still their full merits can only be tested by the works in that country. Murillo and Velazquez are, indeed, everywhere well known; although it is more than suspected that a multitude of the works attributed to the former master are by his pupils Villavicencio, Meneses, and others. The great works of Cano and Zurbaran àre characterized

* This is contradicted by the Editor of the Louvre Catalogue, who says that, from correspondence between Titian and Aretin, the fact of his not being in Spain, at the time asserted. is proved.

by devotional fervour, pure and noble treatment, and by a vigorous and truthful pencil.

The name of Josef Ribera should not be omitted; for though he settled in Naples, and is ranked amongst Italian artists, his *agnomen*, "Lo Spagnoletto," tells of his country equally as his works evince a Spanish treatment or feeling.

It is curious, in tracing the history of art and its migrations, to find that Spanish influence gave birth to a school in Mexico. Sir Edmund Head quotes from a letter of Madame Calderon de la Barca:—"In some of the convents (in Mexico) there still exist, buried alive like the inmates, various fine old paintings; amongst others, some of the Flemish school, brought to Mexico by the monks at the time when the Low Countries were under Spanish dominion." The names of Enriquez, Cabrera, and others, are given as native Mexican artists of very great ability.

MODERN SCHOOLS.

Regarding the history of art as a whole, it has been the custom to call the masters of the Fifteenth, Sixteenth, and Seventeenth Centuries moderns; but as we pass on to the Nineteenth Century they become ancient to us, and we find it necessary to draw the line of distinction between them and the masters properly recognised by us as moderns. The close of the seventeenth century seems the most appropriate period to fix as the conclusion of the art era, which has been briefly sketched in the foregoing pages; and of which the influences are traced through the various European schools. For the most part mediocrity may be said to be the characteristic of the art of the eighteenth century; especially in those countries on the Continent of Europe where the greatest previous development of art had obtained. Towards its close, and early in the present century, a new spirit seems to have awoken, indicating, in some countries, an art revival, or new art epoch. At home the history of art, as a native development, must date from the commencement of the eighteenth century. It has been almost simultaneous in Ireland, England, and Scotland. Previous to 1766 no distinct school existed, although from the revival of the arts in the sixteenth century, native portrait painters existed in England. The majority of distinguished artists were foreigners, invited principally by the reigning monarchs, living apart from the native artists, and certainly forming no distinct schools.

Hans Holbein, a native of Basle,* lived and practised in England during Henry the Eighth's reign. The most distinguished foreigners who painted in England, after him, were Cornelius Jansens, Daniel Mytens, Rubens, Vandyck, Lely, and Kneller. The two latter, though foreigners, almost rank among the English School. Amongst the native artists of this period were the two Olivers; Isaac, who flourished about the latter part of the reign

* Dr. Kugler says he was born at Augsburg.

of Queen Elizabeth, and studied under Zucchero; and Peter, his son, who painted several works for James I. Walker was the distinguished portrait painter of Cromwell and his contemporaries. Dobson, who died prematurely in 1646, was styled the Father of the English School of Portrait Painting. After him came Riley, Richardson, Hudson, Sir James Thornhill, who painted the frescoes in St. Paul's and the hall at Greenwich Hospital; and William Hogarth, the most original genius of his time, whom Walpole describes rather as "a writer of comedy with a pencil than as a painter."

The Royal Academy of London was established under the presidency of Sir Joshua Reynolds in 1768. Among its original constituent members were two Irish artists, George Barrett, a native of Dublin, who exhibited great talent for landscape painting—daring to think for himself and study nature in the picturesque neighbourhood of Powerscourt, although his distinguished friend, Edmund Burke, is said to have urged him rather to study pictures;—and James Barry, a native of Cork, an historical painter of great genius, as his works in the Society of Arts, Adelphi, and elsewhere, attest. The records of his life exhibit him as a man of very eccentric habits, of indomitable energy, struggling against public apathy towards high art—a man before his time.

Both these artists had taken prizes offered for the promotion of Art by the Royal Dublin Society, whose schools were established in 1746, and materially tended to stimulate and educate the native art-mind of Ireland. Bindon, Latham, and others, practised portrait painting, in Dublin, early in the eighteenth century. Very many native artists of merit sprung up, although for the most part they went over to England, and so merged in the English School. Amongst these were Tresham, Peters, and Hamilton; the two former became members of the Royal Academy of London; Sir Martin A. Shee, a pupil of the same school, became its President; Hamilton settled in Ireland. Although several societies of artists were formed, it was not till 1823 that a charter of incorporation was given to the Royal Hibernian Academy.

Drawing schools were first established in Edinburgh in 1707; but the Royal Scottish Academy was not founded until 1838. George Jamieson, a pupil of Rubens, was the first painter noticed in the Scottish annals; Sir Henry Raeburn, the greatest portrait painter Scotland has produced; Sir David Wilkie, its pride and honour.

Wilson and Gainsborough, contemporaneously with Barrett, developed in England the gusto for landscape painting—a branch of art which, since their time, has gradually expanded in practice in these countries, until it has reached a very high degree of excellence, and forms one of the great features of the English School. Portrait painting has also been prominently developed; history, in its highest acceptation, having never been much cultivated, although within the last ten or fifteen years a greater demand seems to have arisen for works of that class.

REGULATIONS

OBSERVED BY PERSONS STUDYING IN THE GALLERIES.

I.—All professional Artists shall be free to copy or study in the National Gallery of Ireland, subject to the regulations as to time, &c., laid down by the Governors and Guardians.

II.—All Art Students, being Students of the Royal Hibernian Academy, shall be admissible on producing a written certificate of qualification from the Keeper of the Academy.

III.—All Students in the Government Schools of Design shall be admissible on producing a certificate of qualification from the Head Masters of such Schools.

IV.—All persons desirous to copy, not being professional Artists, or Students in the R. H. Academy, or any School of Design, will be required to produce some work of their own execution as an evidence of qualification, and shall be admissible on approval by the Director.

V.—All applications for permission to study must be made officially to the Director; in the cases of Students or Amateurs, accompanied by the necessary certificate or specimen.

VI.—In all cases, *measuring* the original picture with any instrument and also all *contact* with it, is strictly prohibited. The persons in charge have directions to prevent such, and to report any breach of this rule; as the safety of valuable works, as well as the true objects of study, can only be secured by its observance.

VII.—No work can be removed from its place on the walls without the special leave of the Director; and if removed, it must be by him, or by some responsible agent of the Institution, with his sanction.

VIII.—All persons painting in the Galleries will be required to provide themselves with proper mats, easels, drawing boards, and stools.

IX.—Persons studying in the Galleries will enter their names in the signature book on each occasion of visiting for the purpose of study.

X.—A bell will be rung a quarter of an hour previous to the termination of the period allotted for study; and all persons studying are expected to have their studies and painting apparatus removed without delay.

INDEX TO THE CATALOGUE

OF

PAINTINGS, WATER-COLOUR DRAWINGS, ENGRAVINGS, AUTOTYPES, &c.

[Memoirs of the Painters will be found at the pages in the Catalogue referred to in margin, and Descriptions of the Subjects follow the Memoirs.]

The Numbers commence in the Principal Gallery at the entrance to the Small Galleries, North Side.

NATIONAL, HISTORICAL, AND PORTRAIT GALLERY.

No.	Subject.	Artist's Name.	Page.
121	Marble Bust of D. Maclise, R.A., .	J. Thomas, . . .	135
122	Portrait of Catterson Smith, R.H.A.,	Himself, ...	101
123	Portrait of the Right Hon. H. Grattan, presented by the Lady Laura Grattan.	T. A. Jones, P.R.H.A., .	62
124	Portrait of 1st Viscount Lifford, .	Robert Lucius West, .	
125	The Volunteers in College Green,	F. Wheally, R.A., . .	112
126	Portrait group of King George II. and family.	W. Hogarth, . . .	60
127	Portrait of Gustavus, Lord Boyne, presented by Mrs. Noseda.	Attributed to Hogarth, .	61
128	Portrait of Edmund Burke, . .	J. Barry, R.A., . . .	38
129	Portrait of Hugh, Duke of Northumberland.	Thomas Gainsborough, R.A.	54
130	Portrait (Bust) of the Most Rev. Dr. Murray.	J. Hogan, R.H.A., . .	60
131	Portrait of the Marquis of Thomond,	Sir Thos. Lawrence, R.A.,	65
132	Portrait of Sir Maziere Brady, Bart., presented by Lady Brady.	T. A. Jones, P.R.H.A., .	62
133	Portrait of Lady Morgan, presented by her Executors.	Berthon, ...	41
134	Bust of Thomas Moore, presented by the Earl of Charlemont, K.P.	C. Moore, R.H.A., . .	73
135	Portrait of Sir H. Lawrence, K.C.B.,	J. T. Dicksee, . . .	50
136	James, Duke of Ormond, presented by the Earl of Carlisle.	Sir P. Lely, . . .	66
137	Portrait of Lord Mount Edgecumbe.	Reynolds (Sir Joshua), .	69
138	Portrait of Dermody the poet, .	C. Allingham, . .	
139	Portrait group of the Sheridan family.	Sir E. Landseer, R.A., .	64
140	Portrait of Sir Thos. Wyse, K.C.B.,	John Partridge, . .	83
141	Portrait of William Dargan, esq., painted for and presented by the Dargan Committee.	Catterson Smith, P.R.H.A.,	101
142	Portrait of Samuel Lover, . .	Harwoo . . .	57
143	Portrait of Arthur, 1st Duke of Wellington.	John Lucas, . . .	69
144	Portrait of C. Moore, R.H.A., . .	John Doyle, . . .	50
145	Portrait (Bust) of the Right Hon. Richard Sheil.	C. Moore, R.H.A., . .	73
146	Small crayon portrait of the Duke of Ormonde.	Sir Peter Lely, . . .	
147	Portrait (in crayon) of Thomas Moore.	G. Richmond, R.A., . .	89
148	Portrait (in crayon) of Clarence Mangan.		
149	Portrait (in crayon) of William Harvey.	} F. W. Burton, R.H.A., .	
150	Portrait (sketch) of Thomas Davis		
151	Portrait (sketch) of Professor J. M'Cullock.		
152	Portrait of Grattan in Indian Ink,	Scott, of Liverpool	

MODERN GALLERY. (B. NORTH.)

No.	Subject.	Artist's Name.	Page.
153	View at Capri, ...	M. G. Brennan, . .	43
154	Judgment of Paris, . . .	Stothard (after Rubens), .	103
155	Interior of a Church, . . .	M. G. Brennan, . .	43
156	Merry Christmas in the Olden Time,	Daniel Maclise, R.A., .	71
157	Landscape Composition, . .	R. Wilson, R.A., . .	112
158	Landscape—Moonlight, . . .	J. A. O'Connor, R.H.A., .	79
159	Portrait, ...	After Sir J. Reynolds, by Martin Cregan, R.H.A., .	48
160	Portrait of Miss Boaden, . .	Harlowe, ...	57
161	Paroquets, ...	E. Murphy, . . .	76
161A	Horse drinking, ...	J. F. Herring, . . .	
162	Opening of the Sixth Seal, . .	F. Danby, A.R.A. and R.H.A.,	49
163	The Dargle, ...	J. A. O'Connor, R.H.A., .	79
164	Glen Isla, ...	Charles Grey, R.H.A., .	56
165	Storm at the entrance of a Mediterranean Port.	Loutherbourg, . . .	69
166	The Blind Piper, presented by the late W. S. O'Brien, esq.	J. Haverty, . . .	58
167	Death of Milo of Crotona, . .	David, ...	50
168	Interior of St. Jacques at Antwerp, presented by the late Earl of Charlemont.	Gennison and Willems, .	54
169	Mortuary Chapel, ...	Herman Dyck, . . .	51
170	Cupid chastised, ...	Prud'hon (attributed to), .	87

GALLERY A. (NORTH.)

Chiefly reserved for Loan Collection.

171	St. Peter and St. John at the Beautiful Gate.	After Raphael's Cartoon, .	97
172	Elymus the Sorcerer struck Blind,	After Raphael's Cartoon, . (Both attributed to Galio Romano.)	97

WATER COLOUR DRAWINGS.

COLLECTION OF WATER COLOUR DRAWINGS BEQUEATHED BY THE LATE
CAPTAIN GEORGE ARCHIBALD TAYLOR.

No.	Subject.	Artist's Name.
	View of Dublin, taken from the spire of St. George's Church in 1853. Mountjoy-square is seen to the left of the foreground; the Rotundo Gardens to the right; Kingstown Harbour appears in the distance, with Sugar-loaf and the distant range of the Dublin Mountains.	James Mahony.
	A Coast Scene, ...	Pritchett.
	The Chapel, Beauchamp Castle, Warwickshire,	J. Mahony.
	Dancing Nymphs, ...	W. E. Frost
	Entrance to Edward the Confessor's Chapel, Westminster Abbey.	J. Mahony.
	Shakespeare's Cliff, Dover, ...	J. Callow.
	A Squall, ...	J. Callow. '
	Interior of a Church, ...	J. Mahony.
	A Shore Scene, ...	Bright.
	A Wood, ...	H. O'Neill.
	La Chiesa di San Benedetto, Subiano, .	J. Mahony.
	Ruins of the Sallyport of Framlingham, . .	W. H. Kearney.
	The Vigil, ...	Ince.
	View near Howth, ...	H. Newton.
	Oliver Cromwell and his Secretary—sketch, .	J. Mahony.
	Quentin Durward's first meeting with Isabelle de Croye at the hostelry, Plessis-le-Tours.	J. Mahony.
	The Menai Straits, near Aber, . . .	Howse.
	Rue Martinville, Rouen, ...	E. Hassell.
	Street Scene in Jersey, ...	H. Newton.
	View in Spain, ...	J. Mahony.
	The Canal side, ...	Mapleson.
	On the Brachlin, Perthshire, . . .	C. Richardson.
	Procession of the Host, ...	Warren.
	Lowestoff, Norfolk, ...	E. Callow.
	Dolbaddern Castle, North Wales, . . .	Howse.
	At Rochester, ...	Howse.
	The Central Hall of the Dublin Exhibition—Queen's private visit.	J. Mahony.
	Scene in the Dungeon—Faust—sketch, . .	T. A. Jones.
	View on the Thames, near Red House, Battersea,	Howse.
	View in Venice, ...	
	Pont-y-Groynd, near Snowdon, . . .	J. C. Bentley.
	Mouth of the Nore, ...	J. C. Bentley.
	Interior of a Church, ...	J. Mahony.
	On the Conway, North Wales, . . .	E. Hassell.
	View in Spain, ...	J. Mahony.
	The Beach at Hastings, ...	Howse.
	Waterfall, co. Wicklow, ...	H. Newton.
	Windsor Castle, ...	Howse.
	Aber, North Wales, ...	Howse.
	View on the Cork River above Monkstown, .	J. Mahony

No.	Subject.	Artist's Name.
	Clock Tower, Rouen, ...	E. Hassell.
	Pont du Paut, on the Sleden, ...	E. Hassell.
	Visit of the Queen and Prince Albert to the Great Dublin Exhibition, 1853.	J. Mahony.
	Ophelia—a sketch—" There's rosemary—that's for remembrance."	T. A. Jones.
	Sea View, ...	Herbert.
	Street View in Rouen, ...	Howse.
	Dover Castle, ...	Howse.
	View near Gorcum, Holland, ...	Howse.
	Interior of Chapel Royal, Dublin Castle, . .	J. Mahony.
	Calais Fish-market, ...	E. Sims.
	The Glen, ...	H. Newton.
	The Rose, ...	Harrison.
	Charles I. preparing for his controversial discussion with the Marquis of Worcester, at Raglan Castle—sketch.	J. Mahony.
	Rochester Castle, ...	Howse.
	St. Malou, Rouen, ...	E. Hassell.
	Faust and Margaret—a sketch, . . .	T. A. Jones.
	Kilgobbin Castle, on the Bandon River, co. Cork,	J. Mahony.
	Waterfall, co. Wicklow, ...	H. Newton.
	Flemish Interior, ...	Howse.
	The Holy Water Font, ...	J. Mahony
	Croix de Pierre, Rouen, ...	E. Hassell.
	River Scene, ...	T. M. Richardson.
	View in Leicestershire, ...	P. Corner.
	La Chiesa di San Cosma e Damino, Roma, .	J. Mahony.
	Mortlake, ...	Howse.
	The Hodman, ...	Phillips.
	View of Sugar-loaf, ...	H. Newton.
	Church of St. Mark, Venice, . . .	J. Mahony.
	London Stone, ...	Howse.
	Le Portrait Charmant, ...	Howse.
	Steam-tug towing a Brig, ...	J. Callow.
	Interior, ...	Howse.
	Boulogne, ...	Howse.
	Grenville Bay, Jersey, ...	J. Callow.
	La Chiesa di Sante Croce at Florence, . .	J. Mahony.
	Prospero allaying the tempest, . . .	J. Mahony.
	Whitby, ...	J. C. Bentley.
	Nella Chiesa di Santa Maria del Popolo, . .	J. Mahony.
	Wimbledon Common, ...	E. Sims.
	I Cognoscenti, ...	Howse.
	The Cavalier, ...	Howse.
	O'Donoghue's White Horse, Killarney, . .	J. Mahony.
	The Irish Mother, ...	Topham.
	Sketch on the Thames, ...	Forde.
	A Windmill, ...	R. P. Noble.
	Esna Lara, Glenariff, near Cushendall, co. Antrim.	H. Newton.
	Blackwall Reach, River Thames, . . .	E. Chambers.
	A Group of Figures, ...	E. B. Campion.
	Sunset, ...	J. C. Buckley.
	Blackrock Castle, ...	J. Mahony.
	West Doorway, Corfe Castle, . . .	Howse.
	Welsh Interior, ...	W. Lee.
	Bell Tower, Rouen, ...	Howse.

No.	Subject.	Artist's Name.
	Sandgate, Kent, ...	J. Callow.
	Sturry, near Canterbury, . . .	Forde.
	Hormonden Green, ...	Gilbert.
	French Cavalry, ...	Hypol. Bellange.
	On the Look-out, ...	Howse.
	View of Berwick-upon-Tweed, . . .	G. C. Bentley.
	Roadside Sketch, ...	Hypol. Bellange.

A portion of this Collection is not hung, for want of space.

SERIES OF WATER COLOUR DRAWINGS OF THE BRITISH SCHOOL, PRESENTED BY WILLIAM SMITH, ESQ., F.S.A.

No.	Subject.	Artist's Name.
	View of St. Vincent's Rock, . . .	Samuel H. Grimm.
	Chinese Junk, ...	William Alexander.
	Woodyard, Windsor Park, . . .	Paul Sandby, R.A.
	Oswestry Church, . . .	Michl. Angelo Rooker, A.R.A
	The North Gate at Yarmouth, .	Michl. Angelo Rooker, A.R.A
	Dane Castle, ...	Thomas Hearne.
	Fountain's Abbey, Yorkshire, . .	Edward Dayes.
	Malmesbury Abbey, . . .	Thomas Hearne.
	View in Hyde Park, . . .	Paul Sandby, R.A.
	From Grey's Elegy, . . .	William Hamilton, R.A.
	The Thames at Battersea, . .	John Varley.
	From Thompson's Seasons, . .	William Hamilton, R.A.
	A country Road, ...	Paul Sandby, R.A.
	St. Alban's Abbey, . . .	J. M. W. Turner, R.A.
	View of St. Asaph, . . .	Thomas Girtin.
	Rustic Scene, ...	Francis Wheatley, R.A.
	View of . . .	Thomas Rolandson.
	The South Gate, Yarmouth, .	Michl. Angelo Rooker, A.R.A
	Southampton Quay, . . .	Edward Dayes.
	An Indian Canoe, . . .	John Webber, R.A.
	Shanklin, Isle of Wight, . .	John Alexander.
	View near Torquay, . . .	D. M. Serres.
	Thanethlede, Wales, . . .	John Webber, R.A.
	View in Hyde Park, . . .	Paul Sandby, R.A.
	The Ponti Salaro, near Rome, .	Richard Cooper.
	Pie Du Midi, ...	John Cozens.
	Jedburgh Abbey, . . .	Thomas Girtin.
	The Tholsel, Dublin, . . .	James Malton.
	Part of the Colosseum, Rome, .	William Marlow
	Eltham Palace, ...	Paul Sandby, R.A.
	Lauffenburgh on the Rhine, . .	William Pars.
	The City of Berne, . . .	William Pars.
	View near Bala, Merionethshire, .	John Webber, R.A.
	Othello and Desdemona, . .	Samuel Shelley.
	Boat and Figures, ...	George Morland.
	Watermouth, Devonshire, . .	Anthony Devis.
	A Landscape, ...	M. A. Rooker, R.A.
	View of the Avon, near Bristol, .	Samuel H. Grimm, esq.
	View of Naples, ...	John Cozens.

LEAVES from a SKETCH-BOOK by J. A. O'CONNOR.

Born in Dublin, 1790 ; died in London, 1840.

THREE WATER COLOURS.

Rochester Castle.
View of Ospringe near Feversham.
On the Beach at Sandgate.

THREE SKETCHES IN SEPIA.

Dover Castle, from the London Road.
Dover, Shakespeare's Cliff in the distance.
Dover Cliff.

One of the Ponds at Hampstead.
A scene on Hampstead Heath.
A group of Pines at Hampstead.
The Boat-house.
Sea-brook near Sandgate, Kent.
A scene in Greenwich Park.
Thames Ditton.
Clifden Rock.
Rownham Ferry, near Bristol.
Part of Clifton Rock.
Botleys.
A scene from Botleys, near Chertsey.

Botleys, near Chertsey.
A sea-brook, near Sandgate.
Break-water, near Tintern.
A view on the Wye.
Caldwell on the Wye.

SEVENTEEN SKETCHES IN PENCIL.

Botleys, west front.
Oaks at Botleys.
East front, Botleys.
North front, Botleys.
A view from the Park, Botleys.
A view from the House, Botleys.
In the Park, Botleys.
Chepstead, on the Wye.
A view on the Wye.
Hampstead.
Botleys.
A scene near Chertsey, Botleys.
Botleys.
Botleys.
A scene from Batleys.
Botleys.
Hampstead.

ORIGINAL DRAWINGS.

INTERMEDIATE (NEW) GALLERY.

FIVE ORIGINAL DRAWINGS presented by HODDER M. WESTROPP, esq.

I. Figure of a Saint writing—black and white chalk, shaded. By Rocca da Perugia. From Cosway and Esdaile collections. 12 in. H., 7½ in. w.
II. Infant Christ and St. John in a landscape—pen outline. By Annibale Carracci. 9¾ in. H., 12½ in. w.
III. Martyrdom of St. Laurence—pen outline. By Domenichino. 9 in H., 11 in. w.
IV. Holy Family—pen outline. By G. Vasari. 12⅓ in. H., 8½ in. w.
V. Study of a Male Head—in black chalk, shaded. By Baroccio. 12 in. H., 8 in. w.

DRAWINGS PURCHASED.

VI. The Last Judgment, part of the design for the Dome of the Cathedral at Parma—red and black chalk. Attributed to Correggio. From Brett collection—two parts. 7½ in. H., 10½ in. w.
VII. The Fall of Phæton—bistre, heightened with chalk. Tintoretto. From Brett collection. 11 in. H., 8½ in. w.
VIII. A Female Head—red chalk. Domenichino. From Brett collection. 4¾ in. square.
IX. Portrait of the Earl of Arundel—Indian ink, slightly coloured. By Vandyck. From the Lawrence and Brett collections. 7½ in. H., 5 in. w.
X. Four heads—black and red chalk—Il Moro, Duke of Milan ; Il Casa Sforza, Francesco Sforza, and Regina Di Casa. By Bassano. Bought at the Brett sale in London. 9 in. H., 6 in. w.

ADDITIONAL PURCHASE FOR 1866.

XI. Virgin seated with Infant Saviour on her lap. Angels on each side playing on musical instruments—in pen and bistre, heightened with white, pricked for the outline. By Guadenzio Ferrari. From Dr. Wellesley's collection. 33 in. H., 21½ in. W.

XII. Portrait of Ludovico Sforza, called Il Moro, highly finished, head life size—in black chalk and wash. By Leonardo da Vinci. From Cosway and Dr. Wellesley's collections. 14 in. H., 9 in. W.

XIII. Head of a young female, nearly life size, circle—pen and sepia. By Lorenzo di Credi. From the collection of Dr. Wellesley. 9 in. diameter.

XIV. A Landscape with trees and buildings along the banks of a wide river, in which vessels are seen; the sun setting over distant mountains. To the right on a rising ground Magdalen praying—pen. By Titian. From the collections of Cosway, Holditch, and Dr. Wellesley. 10¾ in. H., 7½ in. W.

XV. Part of the triumphs of Julius Cæsar. Soldiers carrying trophies —pen and sepia. By Mantegna. From the collections of Lord Spencer, M. Esdaile, and Rev. Dr. Wellesley. 10 in. H., 10½ in. W.

XVI. Life-sized head, profile of young man in a cap—black chalk, outlines pricked, the head subsequently cut out, but carefully inlaid; on the reverse a study of feet. By Antonio Pollajuolo. From the Wellesley collection. 13¾ in. H., 11¾ in. W.

XVII. Landscape. Night effect, a road to the left, a bank to the right with trees and herbage—highly finished in chalk and wash. By Elzheimer. From the collections of Hibbert, Esdaile, and Dr. Wellesley. 5¾ in. H., 10¼ in. W.

XIX. Apollo—in red chalk, apparently a study from a youth posed as the Apollo. By Correggio. From Dr. Wellesley's collection. 13 n. H., 7½ in. W.

XX. Cupid seated fondling an Eagle—in red chalk. By Correggio. On the back studies of two figures for the Dome of Parma. From the collections of Benjamin West, Richardson, and Dr. Wellesley, 5¾ in. H., 3¾ in. W.

XXI. A Rabbit, highly finished—wash and pen in bistre. To the left is written, Albrecht Dürer in Nüremberg. From Dr. Wellesley's collection. 7¾ in. H., 5¾ in. W.

XXII. Figure of a man; in his right hand a book which rests upon his knee, looking to the right. Probably a prophet or evangelist— in pen. By Raphael. From the Lawrence collection. 10 in. H., 5 in. W.

Four Drawings, presented by F. W. Burton Esq., R.H.A.

XXIII. The Virgin's visit to St. Elizabeth—in wash. By Andrea del Sarto. From the Lawrence collection. 9 in. H., 11½ in. W.

XXIV. Study of a kneeling figure, fallen prostrate—in red chalk. By F. Primaticcio. From the Lawrence collection. 5 in. H., 7½ in. W.

XXV. Studies of drapery—in red and white chalk. By F. Primaticcio. From the Lawrence collection. 8 in. H., 6 in. W.

XXVI. Studies of nude male figures. By F. Primaticcio. From the Lawrence collection. 6 in. H., 7½ in. W.

School of Athens. After Raphael.
Sketch of a Greenwich Pensioner. By T. Gainsborough, R.A.
Sketches on the same sheet of paper. By Sir E. Landseer, R.A., Sir George Hayter, and Martin Cregan, R.H.A.

NATIONAL HISTORICAL, AND PORTRAIT GALLERY—(ENGRAVINGS).

No.	Subject.	Painter.	Engraver.
	King William III., .	Sir Godfrey Kneller, .	J. Smith.
	Queen Mary, . .	Sir Godfrey Kneller, .	J. Smith.
	Sir Robt. Southwell, Kt.,	Sir Godfrey Kneller, .	J. Smith.
	Mr. Moody, the actor, .	—	T. Hardy.
	William Congreve, .	Sir Godfrey Kneller, .	J. Smith.
	The Right Hon. Joseph Addison.	Sir Godfrey Kneller, .	J. Smith.
	King James II., . .	Sir Godfrey Kneller, .	J. Smith.
	Second Duke of Ormond.	Sir Godfrey Kneller, .	J. Smith.
	Lord Lucan, 1788, .	Sir Joshua Reynolds,	John Jones.
	Sir William Petty, Kt.,	J. Clostewnan, .	J. Smith.
	—	Sir Joshua Reynolds,	J. R. Smith.
	Sir Richard Steele, .	J. Richardson, 1712,	J. Smith.
	Oliver Goldsmith, . .	Sir Joshua Reynolds,	Jos. Marchi.
	Laurence Sterne, . .	Sir Joshua Reynolds,	J. Fisher.
	Rt. Hon. Edmund Burke,	Sir Joshua Reynolds,	James Watson.
	Duke of Leinster, . .	Sir Joshua Reynolds,	John Dixon.
	Rt. Hon. Henry Grattan.	F. Wheatley, . .	V, Green.
	Dr. John Hoadly, Arch bishop of Dublin.	Isaac Whood, 1733, .	T. Faber.
	The Right Hon. Anthony Malone.	Sir Joshua Reynolds,	J. R. Smith.
	George Marquis Towns-end.	Sir Joshua Reynolds,	C. Turner.
	Daniel O'Connell, . .	J. Haverty, . .	W. M. Ward.
	Arthur, Duke of Wellington.	Sir T. Lawrence, .	Samuel Cousins.
	—	Sir Joshua Reynolds,	John Jones.
	Rt.Hon.Richard Brinsley Sheridan,	Sir Joshua Reynolds,	John Hall.
	Mr. Quin, the actor, .	Thomas Hudson, .	John Faber.
	Right Hon. Hely Hutchison.	Sir Joshua Reynolds,	James Watson.
	Carolan, Irish Bard, .	—	J. Martin.
	Lord Plunket, . .	R. Rothwell, . .	—
	Mrs. Woffington, . .	A. Pond, . . .	James M'Ardel.
	Sir P. Crampton, Bart., .	Catterson Smith, .	—
	Marquis Wellesley, .	Sir T.Lawrence,P.R.A.	—
	Charles Kendal Bushe, .	W. Stevenson, .	D. Lucas.
	Sir R. Mayne, K.C.B., .	—	L. Gruner.
	C. Lucas, M.D., . .	Sir Joshua Reynolds,	James M'Ardel.
	William Sharman Crawford, esq., M.P.	John P. Knight, R.A.,	Thomas Lupton.
	The Right Hon. J. Philpot Curran.	J. B. Lane, . .	S. Freeman.
	The Earl of Charlemont, Duke of Leinster, . .	— Sir Martin Shee, .	— —
	Viscount Castlereagh, .	Sir T.Lawrence,P.R.A.	—
	The Right Hon. George Canning.	Sir T.Lawrence,P.R.A.	—
	The Volunteers of Ireland,	F. Wheatley, R.A.	J. Collyer.

No.	Subject.	Painter.	Engraver.
	Installation Dinner at the Institution of the Most Illustrious Order of St. Patrick, in St. Patrick's Hall, within the Dublin Castle, 17th March, 1783.	J. K. Sherwyn,	J. K. Sherwyn.
	The Siege of Athlone, 1691. (A rare print.)	Johanus Langena,	—

CHROMO LITHOGRAPHS CHIEFLY FROM THE ARUNDEL SOCIETY.

No.	Subject.	Name of Artist.
	The Fall, ...	Filippino Lippi.
	Expulsion, ...	Masaccio.
	St. Peter Preaching, . . .	—
	Christ and St. Mary Magdalane, . .	Fra Angelico.
	The Last Supper, ...	Ghirlandajo.
	St. Anthony, ...	Titian.
	St. Peter and St. Paul, . . .	Masaccio and Filippino Lippi.
	St. Francis Preaching, . . .	Giotto.
	Mount Parnassus, ...	Raphael.
	The Crucifixion, ...	l'ietro Perugino.
	Death of St. Francis, . . .	Dom Ghirlandajo.
	Preaching of St. John the Baptist, .	Dom Ghirlandajo.
	The Fall, ...	Filippino Lippi.
	The Ecstasy of St. Catherine, . .	San Domenico.
	The Figure of the Saviour, . .	Gianantonio.
	St. Peter and St. Paul before Nero, .	Filippino Lippi.
	Angel, ...	Metzzo Da Forli.
	The Presentation in the Temple, .	Luini.
	St. Peter in Prison, . . .	Marianicci.
	Two Heads of Saints, . . .	Ghirlandajo
	St. Peter and St. John, . . .	Marianicci.
	The Raising of St. Petronella, . .	Marianicci.
	Two Heads, ...	—
	Heads of St. Peter and St. Paul, .	—
	St. Peter and St. John, . . .	Masolino.
	The Apostles John and Peter, . .	Albert Durer.
	The Madonna, ...	Hans Holbcin.
	The Prophet Jeremiah, . . .	Michael Angelo.
	St. Peter Baptized, ...	Masolino.
	Jesus and His Disciples at Emmeaus, .	Fra Bartolomeo.
	St. Peter and John Healing the Sick by their Shadows.	—
	Christ taken down from the Cross, . .	Fra Angelico da Fiesole.
	Annunciation, ...	—
	Giottos Chapel at Padua, . . .	—
	The Adoration of the Lamb—Tryptich with four wings.	Jan Van Eyck.
	Adoration of the Magi, ...	Hans Hemling.
	Entombment, ...	Quintin Matsys.

Autotypes from the frescos of Michael Angelo in the Sistine Chapel.
Autotypes from the statues of the Medici Tomb.

ALPHABETICAL CATALOGUE

OF

ARTISTS.

CATALOGUE.

☞ *This Catalogue is arranged on the model of those of the* Louvre *and* National Gallery, London, *Alphabetically, according to the* NAMES OF PAINTERS. *After the short memoir of each Painter will be found the title and particulars of the picture or pictures by or attributed to him. The dimensions of pictures given in this Catalogue are exclusive of frames.*

Reference should be made from the Names on the Frames to the same in the Catalogue, or from the Numbers to those in the Index.

A reference is also made to the portion of the Gallery in which the pictures will be found if not in the large Gallery.

National Historical and Portrait Gallery—Gallery C, south. Modern Gallery—Gallery B, north.

It is perhaps needless to observe that the short descriptive notes where they occur are intended chiefly for the information of those into whose hands the catalogue may fall, who have not the opportunity of seeing the pictures themselves.

ALTDORFER (ALBERT); born, 1488, at Altdorf, near Landshuth, in Bavaria; died, 1538, at Ratisbon.

He was one of the most important and original of Albert Durer's scholars. His principal work is in the Munich Gallery, Cat. No. 169, representing the Victory of Alexander the Great over Darius. The landscape in his works rivals that of his contemporaries of the Netherlands, Patenier and others. Other works of his are to be found in the Chapel of St. Maurice, at Nuremberg, in the Augsburg Gallery, and in Ratisbon. He was also eminent as an engraver. According to Bartsch he was born in 1440, and died in 1533.

6. *Portrait of Count Montfort and Roetenfels.*
1 ft. H., 8 in. W. On panel.

The count is represented here with a mantle and chain of office, looking to the right, and holding the keys of a city, or castle, in his hand. He wears a slouched hat of the period, on which is a monogram. An inscription attached at foot, in German, is to the following effect:—" John, Count of Montfort' and Rotenfels, Royal Privy Councillor and Ambassador, 1523." A very highly finished landscape—background shows a town in front, a chateau or castle on the sloping high grounds, and dark hanging woods on the mountain side.

Purchased in Paris in 1866.

AMERIGHI, or MORIGI, (MICHEL ANGIOLO), called IL CARAVAGGIO; painter and engraver; born at Caravaggio, near Milan, in 1569; died at Porto Ercole in 1609. *Lombard School.*

His father, who was a mason, brought him to Naples at the age of 12 or 15. While assisting him to prepare the walls for the fresco painters, the young Amerighi conceived the project of becoming himself a painter, and soon contrived (it has been said, without any instruction) to be able to paint portraits. He went to Venice after a while, and there studied Giorgione, adopting, at the commencement of his course, that subdued style of shadow which he had learned from the works of that great master, and in which some of the most highly prized works of Caravaggio are executed. He then went to Rome, and very soon became the head of the *Naturalisti* School, taking nature exclusively as the model to be followed, and rejecting with disdain and violence all the doctrines of Raphael, M. Angelo, Carracci, and those who chose to look for something spiritual in that nature. Forced by poverty to assist the Cavalier d'Arpino in some of his works, he soon became his rival and enemy. Caravaggio's character was sombre, ferocious, envious, and quarrelsome; he was forced to fly from Rome on account of a homicide which he committed there, and he then settled in Naples, where he long resided. Subsequently he went to Malta, and, after having been given the Cross by the Grand Master, for the talent displayed in a picture of the decollation of St. John, in the oratory of the Church of the Conventuals there, he quarrelled with one of the Knights, and was thrown into prison. He succeeded, however, in escaping, and resided for some time in Sicily, but died of a malignant fever before he could again reach Rome. He left numerous works in all these places. He had always a great number of admirers and followers, gained by his original and vigorous style, particularly his extraordinary relievo, and a certain often strange grandeur, which caused his other defects to be pardoned. His principal success was in the representation of the manners of the lower classes—musicians, gipsies, drinking parties, feasts, conjurors—and nightly broils and quarrels, in which he himself was no stranger, and by which he is said to have rendered his life scandalous. He exercised a great influence over his cotemporaries, and even on already celebrated artists. Ribera and Guercino studied his works, and Lionel Spada, Manfredi, Carlo Saracini, Valentin, and Simon Vouet were his pupils or imitators. His school does not afford a single instance of a bad colourist, however it may be accused of neglect in design and grace.

79. *Saint Sebastian, after Martyrdom.*

5 ft. h., 4 ft. 2 in. w. On canvas.

The martyred Saint has been taken down from the tree to which he had been bound, and is tended by a female, probably St. Irene, and supported by an aged man, whose head is seen to the left of the spectator. The nude figure painted with singular force and freedom. The whole picture in fine condition.

Presented by His Grace the late Duke of Leinster.

ANGELO, (Michel). [See BUONAROTTI, No. 114–118.]

ANTOLINEZ, (Don Josef); born at Seville, 1639; died at Madrid, 1676. *Spanish School.*

At an early age he was sent to Madrid, to study under Don Francisco Rizi, one of the painters of Philip IV. Painted History, Sacred Subjects and Portraits; the landscapes introduced with his figures were much admired. In the Church of Magdalena, at Madrid, there are two pictures by this master, favourably spoken of by Palomino, representing the "Miraculous Conception" and the "Good Shepherd."

18. *St. Peter liberated from Prison.*

5 ft. 5¾ in. h., 4 ft. 1 in. w. On canvas.

The figures are nearly life-size, and occupy the whole field of the canvas, leaving but little background. An Angel, in varied coloured drapery, stoops over Saint Peter, who looks up amazed, and with outstretched hands. On a cartel on the wall above Saint Peter's head, is inscribed Josef-Antolinez.

Purchased in Dublin, in 1859.

ASPER, (Hans); born at Zurich in 1499 ; died 1571. *German School.*

He was a contemporary, according to Adolph Siret, a pupil, of Hans Holbein the younger, whose manner he imitated with great success ; his portraits were highly esteemed, and are much sought after ; but his reputation is less than it deserves, because many of his works are attributed to Holbein. He also painted charming subject pictures. He was made a member of the great council of Zurich in 1545, and his compatriots struck a medal in his honour; yet he died poor. Two of his sons, Hans Rodolph and Rodolph, practised painting, and their works have been confounded with those of their father. In the Belvedere at Vienna, there is a portrait of a young man by Asper, one also, signed, in Munich, and portraits of Zuinglius and his wife, in Zurich.

21. *Portrait of Margaret Knoblauchin of Zurich*

1 ft. 8 in. H., 1 ft. 2 in. w.　On panel.

The lady, with hands crossed, looks out of the picture towards her right ; her face painted with great delicacy of drawing and finish, and exhibiting very strong individuality of character, with a charming simplicity of expression. She wears a rich crimson dress, with a white under-dress coming up to her throat, richly embroidered in gold. The dress is embroidered also with gold and jewels ; rich rings are on her fingers, and on her head a marvellously embroidered gold cap. A background with mountain and lake scenery, and towns upon the border of the lake, is finished with the wonderful detail which distinguished Asper's fancy works. On the back of the panel are painted the family arms, the chief feature being a great clove of garlick—in German Knoblauch, whence doubtless the family name—an inscription below Katherina Knoblauchin, " yr es alters xix., MDXXXII.　On a shield in one corner, the letter A, possibly the monogram of the artist.

Purchased at the sale of the late Mr. Farrer in London, 1866, in whose collection was a companion picture, portrait of Friederich Rorbach, bearing same date, 1532 ; he was probably Margaret's husband.

BARBIERI, (Giovanni Francesco) ; called Il Guercino; born at Cento, a small town in the province of Bologna, 8th February, 1591 ; died in 1666. *Bolognese School.*

He was styled Guercino in consequence of the injury to one of his eyes. His first master was Paolo Zagnoni, a mediocre painter in Bologna. He is known to have taken lessons from Cremonini. He did not enter the school of the Caracci ; but he studied the works of Ludovico, whom he admired much, and formed for himself a vigorous style. The high esteem in which his works were held in Italy, and the numerous commissions which he obtained, forced him to decline the proffered honour of being Chief Painter to the Kings of England and France. He passed two years in Rome, but returned to his native place in 1642, where he had already established an academy, enriched with a collection of casts from the antique, which was much frequented by Italian and foreign artists. He had great facility and power of execution; but changed his style from a forcible Caravaggiesque manner to a somewhat feeble imitation of the manner of Guido.

71. *St. John in the Desert.*

4 ft. H., 3 ft. w.   On canvas.

The Saint is here represented in the act of preaching, seated, with his right hand upraised, and his countenance towards the spectators. The figure is half length, life size, and a scarlet drapery thrown over the knees. From the collection of the Marquis Campana, Rome.

Purchased in Rome in 1864.

BARRY, (JAMES, R.A.) ; born 1741 ; died, 1806. *British School.*

Was the son of a ship master of Cork, where he was born in 1741. Showed genius for art at an early age, and was allowed to follow his bent, being sent to Dublin to study under Mr. West, then Master of the Schools of the Royal Dublin Society, where he gained the prize for historical painting at the age of 22. His merit attracted the notice of his great countryman Edmund Burke, through whose kindness he was enabled to travel in Italy, where he studied, in Rome and in the Academy of Bologna, of which he became a member. On his return he settled in London in 1770, and devoted himself to painting subjects of a high and imaginative aim, caring little for money. A few years subsequently he offered to paint gratuitously the great room of the Society of Arts, with subjects of heroic size, and actually accomplished this great work, upon which his reputation chiefly rests, within three years, and they form a noble monument of genius and industry. In 1777 he became a Royal Academician, and a few years later was elected Professor of Painting at the Academy. He engraved many of his own works with great vigour and spirit. He died in 1806.

128. *Portrait of the Right Hon. Edmund Burke,*

Statesman, orator, writer, patriot, and philosopher ; born 1729 ; died, 1797.

5 ft. 2 in. H., 3 ft. ¼ in. w.

Three-quarters length, in deep chocolate coloured dress ; right hand resting on table, left on hip, looking to left ; curtain and bookshelves in background. The face expressive of great power, apparently a more literal likeness than the portraits by Reynolds. The picture was exhibited at the Royal Academy the year of the artist's election a member.

Purchased for the Gallery, in London, 1875. (In Historical and Portrait Gallery.)

BASSANO, IL.   [See PONTE, Nos. 27, 33, 41, 44, 45, 122.]

BEGA, or BEGYN, (CORNELIS) ; painter and engraver ; born at Haarlem, 1620 ; died of the plague in the same city, 27 August, 1664. *Dutch School.*

His father, Peter Begyn, a sculptor, placed him in the school of Adrian Von Ostade, whose style he fully adopted in depicting the amusements and drolleries of Dutch peasant life. If he did not equal his master, in point of execution he was not far inferior to him, and his works are highly esteemed in private collections, although but few are to be found in public galleries. He is said to have led an irregular life, which forced him from the paternal mansion, and induced his change of name. Whatever his early delinquencies may have been, he met his death in a manner which did him honour, if, as it is said, he was seized with the plague while tending a young person with whom he was on the eve of marriage, and who, when attacked by this fearful disorder in 1664, was deserted by every one but the painter, Bega. He is entitled to notice, also, as an engraver, and left some thirty-four or thirty-five plates, executed with spirit and ingenuity, after him.

28. *Two Men Singing—an Interior.*

1 ft. 1½ in. H., 1 ft. w. On panel.

Two men are leaning over a piece of music singing, evidently to the top of their voices; around are strewed musical books and instruments. Painted with the blackish tone characteristic of the master, with high and careful finish. In a pure state.—Signed C. BEGA, 1662.

Purchased in London in 1863; formerly in Mr. Wm. Hope's collection.

BELLINI, (GIOVANNI); born in Venice in 1422; died there in 1516. *Venetian School.*

This illustrious artist, who may be said to have been the father of the Venetian school, was son of Jacopo Bellini, a painter, not indeed without merit, but who still adhered to the hard, conventional style of his predecessors and cotemporaries. Giovanni soon sought to emancipate himself from this dry manner, and infused more of nature and refinement, with a richer feeling of colour, into his works. The discovery of oil painting, or its admirable perfection, achieved by the Van Eycks early in the fifteenth century, wrought a great revolution in European art. Antonello da Messina is reported to have made himself master of the art under the Van Eycks; his works, still extant, are undoubted evidence of his mastery. From him Giovanni Bellini is said to have acquired the secret of the use of oil colours, and thus attained a range of power and varied attractiveness denied to the practitioner in simple tempera. No doubt the transition from tempera painting, which always involved a pure white ground and previous thorough preparation for the work to be executed, facilitated the early oil painters in the richness and purity of execution. They obtained thereby luminousness of effect, which, coupled with the certainty of touch which the mastery of hand and thought gives, secured to their works brilliancy and durability. Giovanni practised much in conjunction with his brother Gentile, and the fame of the brothers was so diffused by their works, that Mahomet I. asked, through the Ambassador of the Republic, one of the brothers for his service. Gentile accepted the mission, as being best adapted to sustain the inconveniences of distant travelling. Many of Bellini's finest works adorned the churches of Venice, and some still remain; but one of the finest, "The Virgin and Infant Christ enthroned with Saints," in the Church of S. Giovanni e Paolo, called San Zanipolo, has been recently destroyed in company with one of Titian's masterpieces, the Peter Martyr. Giorgione and Titian were the illustrious pupils of Giovanni, who in his advanced years did not disdain to improve his style by the study and adaptation of the manners of his own disciples. In the later years of his life he cultivated portrait-painting to a great extent, and the most illustrious sovereigns, statesmen, and men of letters were the subjects of his pencil. To his industry and high position in his art when even approaching his ninetieth year, a graceful testimony is borne by Albert Durer, who, being in Venice, writes of Giovanni, "He is old, exceedingly old; nevertheless none of the Venetian painters can vaunt themselves on being as vigorous (*vert*) as he." He was employed on a work for the Duke of Ferrara, a group of Bacchanalians, in the year 1516; when, in his ninetieth year, he died. Titian is said to have sought to complete this work with the zeal and devotion of an admiring pupil, and no doubt other works unfinished at Bellini's death were completed by Titian and Giorgione. Giovanni was interred in the Church of S. Giovanni e Paolo.

100. *Portraits of Two Venetian Personages.*

2 ft. 1 in. н., 3 ft. 2 in. w. On panel.

A Venetian Noble or Senator, wearing a robe of cloth of gold, lined with ermine, and a black cap, looks, seemingly in conversation, towards a gentleman wearing the gown of some charitable confraternity, holding a red cap in his hand. Nothing is known as to the identity of the persons represented, the only clue being an inscription on the back of the panel as follows :—

"Beazzano et Navagero poetes,"

with the name of Giorgione, the date of which is unknown, but probably not earlier than the time when the picture formed part of the collection of Cardinal Fesch. Beazzano was highly esteemed as a statesman as well as a poet, and was trusted by the Venetians as an envoy to Rome. He is recorded as having been in Venice in 1514, intimately engaged with Bembo, afterwards cardinal, for whom Bellini painted several pictures of his friends. In later times the picture has been ascribed to Giovanni Bellini. It is no doubt in reality the joint production of both masters, having probably been commenced by the elder and finished by his pupil the younger painter. The difference of style and manipulation in the painting of the two figures is striking. The one exhibiting all the masterly freedom and glowing tones of Giorgione, while the other shows the dry, careful, and stippled touch of Bellini. The picture was brought to Paris from the Fesch sale by M. Aguado ; subsequently was purchased by Count Pourtales, and by him presented to Paul Delaroche, who preserved it until his death. It was purchased at his sale in 1857, by M. Augniot, Paris, from whom it was bought for the National Gallery of Ireland, in 1867.

BELLOTTO, (BERNARDO, called CANALETTO) ; born at Venice, 1724; died at Warsaw, 1780. *Venetian School.*

He was a pupil of his uncle, Antonio Canal (called Canaletto), and imitated his manner. Bernardo travelled through Italy, where he painted the most remarkable buildings of the different towns ; he then went to Vienna, afterwards to the court of Dresden, and finally to Warsaw. He is known in England by the name Canaletto, and in Germany as the Count Bellotti.

73. *Landscape.   View of Meissen.*

2 ft. 4 in. н., 3 ft. 11½ in. w. On canvas.
Presented to the Gallery by ROBERT CLOUSTON, Esq.

BENOZZO. [See GOZZOLI, No. 4.]

BERGEN (DIRK, or THEODORE, VAN) ; born at Haarlem, 1645 ; died, 1689. *Dutch School.*

He was a pupil of Adrian Van den Velde; painted landscapes and cattle; and although he never equalled his master in reputation, his best works are frequently attributed to Van den Velde. He settled in London about 1673; but returned to his native country.

59. *The Old White Horse.*

1 ft. 11 in. H., 1 ft. 8½ in. w. On canvas.

An old white horse stands in an enclosed landscape, with cattle and sheep around him ; a shepherd and female are seated in the background, in conversation.

Formerly in the collection of M. Zachary ; purchased in London at the Anderson Sale in 1864.

BERRETINI (PIETRO), DA CORTONA ; commonly called PIETRO DA CORTONA ; a painter, architect, and writer ; was born at Cortona, 1st November, 1596, and died at Rome, 16th May, 1669. *Roman School.*

Though this artist was a Florentine by birth, he belongs more to the Roman School as a painter. At the age of 13 he left Florence and his first master, **Andrea Commodi**, to repair to Rome, where he entered the studio of Baccio Ciarpi, a Florentine painter. The works of Raphael, of M. Angelo, and of Polidoro, the antique statues, and particularly the bas-reliefs of the column of Trajan, became objects of assiduous study to him. He painted for Urban VIII., and afterwards was employed in the Barberini Palace, upon a great work, which may be called his *chef d'œuvre.* He subsequently travelled in Lombardy and in the Venetian States ; and after having painted for some time in the Pitti Palace, in Florence, returned to Rome. Here he proceeded to destroy what he had previously done, and re-painted the Barberini Palace, besides executing a great number of frescoes, as well as easel pictures. He was created a Knight of the Golden Spur, by Alexander VII. During his life he enjoyed an immense reputation, and he left considerable property after him. He was buried in the Church of St. Martin, of which he was the architect, and to which he left a legacy of 100,000 crowns. Lanzi says of him, that he is reckoned the inventor and chief artist of a style which, in the opinion of Mengs, combines facility with taste ; and that his skill in foreshortening, in the disposition of his figures, and the play of light, must always fascinate the soul. A crowd of painters followed his manner, which, however, afterwards degenerated into negligence and affectation. His principal pupils were Romanelli, Ciro Ferri, Pietro Testa, and Giordano.

75. *Death of Lucretia.*

3 ft. 2 in. H., 4 ft. 6 in. w. On canvas.

The moment selected by the artist is that in which Lucretia has just plunged the fatal dagger into her bosom. Her husband, Collatinus, clasps his hands, as he leans forward towards her in horror. Behind stands another helmeted warrior.

Purchased in Rome, in October, 1856, for the National Gallery of Ireland.

BERTHON (RENE THEODORE) ; born, 1778, at Tours. *French School.*

133. *Portrait of Lady Morgan.*

(In Historical and Portrait Gallery.)

4 ft. 3 in. H., 3 ft. 2½ in. w.

Painted in 1808. Bequeathed by the late Lady Morgan to the Nation, and presented by her Executors to the National Gallery of Ireland.

BLOEMEN, or BLOOM, (John, or Julius Francis, Van), called Orizonte; painter and engraver; born at Antwerp in 1656; died at Rome in 1748 or 1749. *Flemish School.*

The name of his master is unknown, as is also the period of his going to Italy. The Academy of Saint Luke at Rome received him among its members, and gave him the title of Orizonte, because he so thoroughly understood and represented the gradations of landscape. At first he imitated the manner of Van der Kabel, then that of Gaspar Dughet or Poussin, but ultimately created a style peculiarly his own. He, particularly, painted the environs of Rome and Tivoli. He was brother of P. Van Bloemen. Another brother, Norbert Van Bloemen, was born at Antwerp in 1672, studied in his own country, then made the voyage of Italy, and died at Amsterdam in 1748. Norbert painted familiar scenes and portraits.

10. *Italian Landscape.*

1 ft. 7 in. h., 3 ft. 1 in. w.

A long flat middle distance, with a river flowing towards the foreground—an Italian villa in the plain, with mountain background. This picture is evidently in Orizonte's second or Gaspar Poussin manner.

Presented by Thomas Berry, Esq., LL.D.

BOL, (Ferdinand); painter and engraver. Born at Dordrecht, about 1610; died at Amsterdam, 1681. *Dutch School.*

Bol was one of the best pupils of Rembrandt, whose manner he imitated with much art, even in his etchings, which are justly esteemed. He painted many historical pieces, and a great number of portraits.

47. *David's Dying Charge to Solomon.* (Kings, ii. 1, 2.)

5 ft. 7½ in. h., 7 ft. 6½ in. w. On canvas.

David, scarcely able to raise his head from his death pillow, places one feeble hand upon the crown and sceptre, while with the other he enforces his admonition to Solomon, who looks upon him from the further side of the bed : " I go the way of all the earth, be thou strong, therefore, and show thyself a man." Bathsheba is seated at the near side. Signed and dated—F. Bol ; fecit, 1643.

A good example of the luminous depth of shadow colour and smooth finish so characteristic of one period of Rembrandt's manner, and which Bol imitated more successfully than any of his other pupils. In a perfectly pure state.

Deposited with the Irish Institution, in 1854, for the National Gallery of Ireland, by the Earl of St. Germans, then Lord Lieutenant.

BORDONE, (Paris) ; born at Treviso, in 1500 ; died in Venice, 1571. *Venetian School.*

He was of noble family, a *cavaliere*, and was a pupil of Titian; but aimed more at the style of Giorgione. He painted history and sacred subjects; but excelled in portraiture. His most celebrated historical work is in the Academy of Venice, "The Fisherman presenting to the Doge the ring received from S. Mark." He was some time in France, where he went on the invitation of Francis I. He painted many public works in Milan, Genoa, and Florence.

82. *Portrait of a man.*

1 ft. 10 in. H., 1 ft. 6 in. w. On canvas.

The expression of the head looking fixedly at the spectator is somewhat stern ; it may, possibly, be a portrait of Bordone himself. Great force and freedom of execution.

Purchased in Paris, in 1867.

BOULOGNE (BON) the Elder ; painter and engraver. Born at Paris in 1649 ; died 16 May, 1717. *French School.*

We find the name differently written—Boullogne, Boullongue ; but Bon always signed himself "Boulogne aine." He was pupil of his father, **Louis de Boulogne**, who, taking advantage one day of a visit of Colbert to the Academy, presented a half figure of St. John, executed by his son, to the Minister, who was much pleased with it, and accorded a pension at Rome to the young painter, although he had not competed for the grand prize of the Academy. He passed five years at Rome, copying the great masters, and endeavouring to adopt their style. He was received in the Academy of France the 27th November, 1677; his picture of reception or diploma-work being Hercules combating the Centaurs (No. 33 in the Louvre Catalogue). He worked at the staircase at Versailles under Le Brun ; painted in fresco, in 1702, the Chapel of St. Jerome in the Church of the Invalides, and many other public works. He has sometimes executed pasticcios in imitation of the great masters. He was extremely laborious, and worked constantly by lamplight. He exhibited in the Salons of 1699 and 1704.

60. *The Call of the Sons of Zebedee.*

10 ft. 4 in. H., 8 ft. 1½ in. w. On canvas. Figures—life size.

Christ stands by the water side, with outstretched hand toward James and John, one of whom is springing from the boat. Zebedee is seated in the boat, and all the countenances are expressive of faith and enthusiasm.

Formerly in the Fesch collection at Rome, where it was brought from France.
Purchased at Rome in 1856, for the National Gallery of Ireland.

BRENNAN, (MICHAEL G.) ; died, 1871.

A native of Sligo. Became a student of the Schools of the Royal Dublin Society, and of the Royal Hibernian Academy, where he early distinguished himself ; subsequently studied in Italy. Exhibited with great success at the Royal Academy. Died in Algiers of consumption, from which he had been suffering for some years, in 1871. A notable loss to Irish art.

153. *View in a Vineyard at Capri—sunset.*

2 ft. 5½ in. w., 1 ft. 10 in. H. (In Modern Gallery.)
Purchased for the Gallery, in London, in 1873.

155. *The interior of a Church at Capri.*

2 ft. 5¼ in. H., 1 ft. 11½ in. w. (In Modern Gallery.)
Purchased for the Gallery, in London, in 1873.

BRUYN, (BARTOLOMAEUS DE); flourished between 1520 and 1550. *School of Cologna.*

The Adoration of the Kings.

2 ft. 2 in. H., 1 ft. 9½ in. w. On panel.

In this picture the Blessed Virgin sits in the porch of a ruin, holding the Infant Christ on her lap ; the Child leans forward to one of the kings, who kneels before him, holding and kissing his hands. St. Joseph stands behind the king. The other kings and their retinue come in through a porch behind the Blessed Virgin and Child on the right. Through the front arch is seen a Rhine landscape with figures.

This picture was in the Krüger collection at Minden, and has also been attributed to Schwartz. (See SCHWARTZ.)

Deposited in the Gallery by the Trustees of the National Gallery of London.

BUONAROTTI, (MICHEL ANGELO).

BRONZINO. [After Michel Angelo's design.]

77. Venus and Cupid.

4 ft. 5¼ in. H., 6 ft. 4 in. w. On panel.

Venus, recumbent, turns to kiss her son, Cupid, from whom she takes an arrow and who springs toward her. His bow and quiver are suspended from a pedestal, from which also hang two coloured masks. A vase of flowers rests upon the pedestal ; landscape and sky background. Of a similar picture by Pontormo, which is in Hampton Court, Mrs. Jameson writes :—

" We have here no voluptuous and attractive queen of loves and graces, but the great goddess of the antique world—the mighty mother of gods and men—the Venus Urania, daughter of Cœlus and Terra, who, when Saturn and the elder gods were dethroned, made way for her younger rival, the Paphian Venus, as Hyperion made way for Apollo."

The original design of this picture was made by Michel Angelo for his friend, Bartolommeo Bettini, to be executed in oil by Jacopo Carucci da Pontormo ; which work is in the Palazzo Colonna, at Rome. More than one of these were painted, as one is said to be in Berlin, and one certainly was brought into England. It was purchased, according to Mrs. Jameson, by Queen Charlotte for £1,000. She mentions another as being in the possession of a Professor D'Alton, of Bonn. The picture No. 118 is believed to be a copy, by Bronzino, whose manner is easily recognizable in it.

Presented by Viscount POWERSCOURT in 1864.

CANALETTO. [See BELLOTTO.]

CARAVAGGIO. [See AMERIGHI.]

CARRACCI, (ANNIBALE); born at Bologna, 3rd November, 1560; died at Rome, July, 1609. *Bolognese School.*

Annibale Carracci was at first destined for his father's business, that of a tailor; but his cousin, Ludovico Carracci, already a painter of great eminence, seeing his inclination and taste for drawing, took him into his own house and educated him carefully in the art. Annibale profited so well by his instructions that he was soon able to assist his master; and, leaving Bologna, he went to Parma, where he studied the works of Correggio; then to Venice, where, becoming personally intimate with Tintoretto and Paul Veronese, he neglected no means of fathoming the secrets of the Venetian colouring. After some time he returned to Bologna, and joined his brother, Agostino Carracci, and his cousin, Ludovico, who generously acknowledged the superiority of his former pupil. The three Carracci there founded a School of Painting which soon became celebrated for its excellence. Annibale was afterwards invited to Rome by the Cardinal Odoardo Farnese, to paint the ceiling of his palace, upon which splendid work he spent eight years; but the injustice done him, in paying but the small sum of 800 crowns for it, affected his professional pride so much, notwithstanding his extreme disinterestedness of character, that he fell into a profound melancholy from which he never recovered. He died soon after at Rome, where he prayed to be buried beside Raphael.

89. *Christ on the Cross.*

10 ft. 3 in. H., 7 ft. 9½ in. W. On canvas.

On the right of the cross, St. Francis; on the left, St. Anthony of Padua; both kneeling. Above, on each side, an adoring angel floating on the clouds, towards the upper part of the cross. This picture was painted by order of the Farnese Family, for a Church in their Bisentine Isle, on the frontier of Naples. It is noted in the "Artistic Memoirs of the House of Farnese." Was subsequently in the possession of Gott, the Sculptor.

Few works of the master show such grand simplicity of conception, or such a sober dignity of execution. The solemn grey tones prevailing through the picture are peculiarly in harmony with the subject. The drawing very noble without being too academic, the master's usual defect.

Purchased in Rome, in 1856, for the National Gallery of Ireland.

CLAESSENS, (ANTONY), the Elder. Fifteenth century. *School of Van Eyck.*

This artist belonged to the latest followers of the Van Eyck School, and is not to be confounded with a younger painter of the same name, belonging to the Dutch School, of about 1550. Two of the elder Claessens' pictures are preserved in the Academy at Bruges, and were formerly in the Town-hall. They represent the Judgment of Cambyses: in the first he causes the unjust judge to be seized, and in the other orders him to be flayed. Both compositions are correct in drawing and powerful in colouring, but deficient in genuine life.

The Nativity.

2 ft. 1½ in. H., 1 ft. 6¼ in. W. On panel: in oil.

The Blessed Virgin kneels, adoring the Infant Christ as he lies on the ground; four angels kneel round him, and three hover in the air over his head. St. Joseph enters with a candle, but perceives that light proceeds from the Child sufficient to illuminate the scene. Two richly dressed persons follow, one holding a lantern ; and in the background the Birth of Christ is announced to both the shepherds and the kings. The dresses in this picture are singular; the Blessed Virgin wearing a robe of a very dark green, almost black ; St. Joseph, red ; and the little angels, long surplices, one of them a priest's cope. When seven angels are represented in this subject by the early painters, they are always understood as the Seven Spirits that stand before the throne of God ; and of these Raphael is always painted wearing the robes of a priest.

Deposited by the Trustees of the National Gallery of London. [Formerly in the Krüger Collection, at Minden.]

CORTONA, (Pietro da). [See Berretini, No. 50.]

COSTANZI, (Placido) ; painter of history ; born at Rome in 1688 ; died, 1759. (Roman School.)

Of his large works that of S. Camillo in S. Maria Madalena is the most esteemed; in it he imitated Domenichino. He also painted in fresco the Tribune in S. Maria in Campo Marzio, and was much employed in painting figures in the landscapes of other artists, particularly in those of Gio. Francesco Van Bloemen, called Orizonte.

Saint Pancrazio with the Infant Christ.

9 ft. 3 in. H., 6 ft. 7 in. w.

At the right, Saint Pancrazio holds the Infant Christ in his arms, while monks in white robes kneel adoring ; the Blessed Virgin, Saint Joseph, and Saint John the Baptist to the right, and angels above. This picture was originally painted for the Church of Saint Pancrazio, in Rome. It became the property of the late Cardinal Fesch, in 1843, on the taking down of this church.

Purchased in Rome, in 1856, for the National Gallery of Ireland.

COTIGNOLA, (Francesco da), called Zaganelli ; flourished about the year 1518 ; school of Parma.

This painter resided chiefly at Ravenna. He was a scholar of Nicolo Rondinello. Both Lanzi and Vasari speak highly of works by Francesco, particularly a "Resurrection of Lazarus," which is at Classe, and a "Baptism of Christ" at Faenza. One of his most extraordinary works is a large altar picture at the Osservanti at Parma, representing the Virgin, with several saints. He had a brother named Bernardino, with whom he painted, in 1504, a picture representing the Virgin between St. Francesco and the Baptist, placed in the interior chapel of the Padri Osservanti in Ravenna; and another at Imola, in the Church of the Reformati, dated 1509. Some have confounded the two brothers, from the names Francesco and Bernardino appearing on the same picture.

106. *The Infant Christ adored by the Virgin and Saints.*

5 ft. 11 in. H., 5 ft. w.   On canvas, transferred from panel.

The Infant Christ is seated on a pedestal ; the Virgin kneels before him at one side, a Franciscan saint behind her ; on the opposite side St. Francis and St. Anthony of Padua. There is an inscription on a cartel on the pedestal, partly obliterated, but apparently attributing the work to Francesco Bernardino Cotignola, dated 7th April, 1509. This may be the work referred to by Lanzi as being at Imola. It was brought to England by Mr. Wigram, and was subsequently in possession of M. Nieuwenhuys.

Purchased in London, in 1864.

COYPEL, (ANTOINE) ; painter and engraver ; born at Paris, 11th April, 1661; died, 7th January, 1722. *French School.*

He was son and pupil of Noel Coypel, who when named Director of the French Academy at Rome, brought him with him, although only eleven years of age. He exhibited talent very early, and devoted himself much to the study of the works of Raphael, of Michel Angelo, and Annibale Carracci. He carried off a prize in the Academy of St. Luke, which insured him the friendship of the Chevalier Bernier and of Carlo Maratti. He obtained other prizes, and executed many works for churches before he was twenty years of age. He was received into the Academy of France in 1681, being scarcely twenty. His diploma picture was Louis XIV. reposing in the arms of glory, after the peace of Nimiguen. He was appointed by the King, in 1710, director of the paintings and drawings belonging to the crown. He was on the point of accepting advantageous offers for visiting England, when he was urged by the Duke of Chartres not to quit France. The Duke subsequently becoming Duke of Orleans, and Regent of the kingdom, appointed him his principal painter, and confided to him the decoration of the new gallery of the Palais Royal, where he painted fourteen subjects taken from the Æneid. As a mark of his approbation of these works, the Duke presented Coypel with a carriage and a pension of 1,500 livres, besides desiring to become his pupil. Coypel made the designs for the medals of Louis XIV., and composed an essay on painting, addressed to his son. His death prevented the completion of a set of compositions from the Iliad and from the Holy Scriptures, intended to be executed in tapestry. He was buried in St. Germain l'Auxerrois. Antoine Coypel produced a great number of works for churches and royal palaces, many of which have been engraved by Poilly, Tardieu, Desplaces, B. Picart, Duchange, Edelinck, Andran, Simonneau, and Drevet. He exhibited in the Salons in 1699 and 1704.

113. *Christ curing one possessed by a Devil.*

11 ft. 10 in. H., 8 ft. 4½ in. w.   On canvas; figures life size.

Christ, standing in the centre of the picture, with hand upraised, exorcises the evil spirit; the man possessed, a figure nearly nude, writhes in agony ; to the right of Christ stands St. John, with arms crossed ; a High Priest and other spectators look on in wonder. Signed A. C. Coypel, anno 1717.

Formerly in the Fesch collection.

Purchased in Rome, in 1856, for the National Gallery of Ireland.

CREGAN (MARTIN, R.H.A.); born, 1788; died, 1870. *British School.*

A native of Dublin, who early distinguished himself as a portrait painter, and gained, and for many years kept, the foremost place in that branch of art in his native city. He was also for many years President of the Royal Hibernian Academy.

159. *Master Crewe.*

12 ft. 11¾ in. w., 2 ft. 3½ in. .

From the celebrated picture by Sir Joshua Reynolds, in the possession of Lord Crewe, and well known from the mezzotint engraving; an admirable example of copying, in which not only the drawing and colour are reproduced faithfully, but also the method of handling.

Purchased for the Gallery, in Dublin, 1871. In Modern Gallery.

CUYP (AALBERT); painter and engraver; born at Dort, 1605; date of his death uncertain living in 1672. *Dutch School.*

He was the son and disciple of Jakob Gerritz Cuyp, whom, however, he far excelled. He painted landscape and cattle, also frequently seaports with shipping, and especially drew the scenes along the banks of the river Maes; but he diversified his style and subjects, painting portrait with great power, and cavaliers on horseback. His pictures are distinguished by luminous atmosphere. Among the many subjects which he painted he particularly succeeded in river scenes and frost pieces, with numerous figures on a small scale. During his life, and for more than a century subsequent to his death, his works were comparatively little valued; since then they have risen enormously in price.

49. *Milking Cows.*

2 ft. 2¼ in. w., 1 ft. 8 in. H.

Formerly in the Gillott Collection. A girl with a straw hat sitting in foreground milking a dun coloured cow; two elaborately finished large brass milk cans, such as they still use in Holland, beside her; other cows and figures in background; beautiful silvery effect. The principal group, including the milk cans, almost identical with that of the large picture in the Bridgewater Collection.

Presented to the National Gallery of Ireland, by JOHN HEUGH, Esq., of Tunbridge Wells.

31. *Small Cattle Piece.*

1 ft. 4½ in. w., 1 ft. 3¼ in. H.

Also from the Gillott Collection. Two cows and some sheep in a marshy landscape, with cloudy sky. The authenticity of this picture is doubtful, the sheep and foreground reminding one more strongly of the manner of Nicholas Berghem.

Purchased for the Gallery in 1873.

44. *A Shooting Party* (attributed to).

2 ft. 8½ in. w., 1 ft. 10¾ in. H. Panel.

A sunny evening effect. A servant in blue dress holding a brown horse, another in red in foreground crouching and holding two dogs; a lady behind on a dun palfrey, shading her eyes from the sun ; a sportsman in the middle distance shooting apparently at sitting game, at which a dog is setting. Large sandy hills in distance, with a chateau in the plain. A rich warm glow of sun, the figures highly finished, but with a free touch.

Purchased for the Gallery, in London, in 1873.

22. *Scene on the Ice; Dort in the Distance.*

1 ft. 6½ in. H., 2 ft. w. Oval; on panel.

Numerous figures are depicted in all the varieties of enjoyment and traffic on the frozen highway. A booth is erected on the ice, in front of which a sledge, full of travellers, is preparing to start ; a woman has fallen just in front, with her basket of eggs rolling on the ice.

Purchased in London in 1864.

DANBY, (FRANCIS, A.R.A. and R.H.A.) ; born at Wexford, 1793 ; died, 1861.

He was a student in the schools of the Royal Dublin Society, and exhibited his first works in Dublin. Went to England in 1819, where he resided at Bristol for some time. Exhibited his first picture at the Royal Academy the following year, after which he rapidly rose in public estimation, excelling in poetical and imaginative landscape; and from that time till his death was a frequent exhibitor. Was early elected an associate of the Academy.

162. *The Opening of the Sixth Seal.*

8 ft. 4½ in. w., 6 ft. 1 in. H.

One of the most famous of the works of the master, exhibiting as it does, in the highest degree, all his best characteristics.

The picture is well known from the engraving ——

Purchased for the Gallery, in London, in 1871.

DAVID, (JACQUES LOUIS) ; born at Paris, 1748 ; died at Brussels, 1825. *French School.*

At twenty-one, David became a pupil of Vien, and after two years (in 1771) he successfully competed for the prize of the French Academy of Rome, the subject being the classic one of the combat of Minerva against Mars and Venus. After some years of labour he accompanied his master, Vien, to Rome, in 1775, upon the appointment of the latter to be Director of the French Academy there ; and during his stay in Rome (until 1780) David devoted himself exclusively to the study of the antique, drawing in outline much oftener than painting. On his return, his picture of Belisarius was accepted at the Academy in Paris, and in 1783 he was elected an Academician on the exhibition of his "Death of Hector." After this he again visited Italy, and subsequently Flanders; and he was appointed Assistant Professor of Painting in July 1792. On the breaking out of the Revolution, however, David resigned the practice of art for a time, to plunge into the exciting scenes of political life, and united himself to the party of Robespierre. He was imprisoned upon the fall of Robespierre, and after having been twice incarcerated for several months, was only released in October, 1795, from which time he renounced politics and applied himself exclusively to his profession for the remainder of his life. On the creation of the Institute of France, David was, with Van Spendonk, appointed to name the first members of the class of the Fine Art, and it was at the Institute that he became at this time acquainted with Napoleon Bonaparte, ever afterwards his friend, and, as Emperor, his patron and supporter. During the Empire he was decorated with the Cross of the Legion of Honour, and during the Hundred Days promoted to be commander in that illustrious Order. But on the restoration of the Bourbons, under the law of proscription of 1816, the great painter was obliged to exile himself from France for ever, at sixty-eight years of age. He then settled at Brussels, where he resided till his death. David was the great support of the Classical Academic School in France, and had numerous disciples, since celebrated among the most distinguished of modern painters; such as Girodet, Drouais, Gros, Gérard, Isabey, Ingres, Leopold Robert, Granet, &c.

167. *The Death of Milo the Crotonian.*

8 ft. h., 6 ft. 3 in. w.   On canvas.

The powerful figure of the Greek athlete is exhibited in an attitude of strained exertion, as he struggles to tear his hand from the split oak tree, which has caught him with irresistible power in his attempt to rend it asunder. Two wolves have seized upon him below ; one of them he has succeeded in trampling on the ground, but the other has fastened himself on his victim.

Presented to the IRISH INSTITUTION, for the National Gallery of Ireland by ARTHUR L. GUINNESS, Esq., 1856.

DICKSEE, (J. T.) of London.

135. *Portrait of Sir Henry Montgomery Lawrence,* K.C.B.

Born in Londonderry, 1806 ; died at Lucknow, 1857.   Statesman and soldier.

3 ft. 1½ in. h., 2 ft. 5½ in. w.

In Historical and Portrait Gallery.

DOMENICHINO.   [See ZAMPIERI, No. 7.]

DOYLE, (JOHN) ; born in Dublin, 1797 ; died, 1868.

Studied in Dublin under Comerford and others. Went to London in 1823, where he soon afterwards commenced the publication of the famous series of political sketches known only by the signature HB, which continued to appear until about 1844. He painted a few portraits in oil.

144. *Portrait of Christopher Moore,* R.H.A.

Born in Dublin, 1790 ; died, 1863.   Sculptor.

1 ft. 11¾ in. h., 1 ft. 7½ in. w.

In Historical and Portrait Gallery.

DYCK, (ANTON VAN); painter and engraver; born at Antwerp, the 22nd March, 1599, died at Blackfriars, London, 10th December, 1641. *Flemish School.*

His father, Frans Van Dyck, a painter upon glass, placed him under Van Balen, in 1610. Subsequently he entered the School of Rubens, and made such rapid progress as to be soon able to aid him in his great works. He was made a member of the confraternity of Saint Luke on the 11th February, 1618. Van Dyck went to Italy in October, 1621, and on his arrival at Genoa, executed a number of portraits which brought him into great repute. In 1622 he went to Rome, where he copied the *chefs d'œuvre;* passed on to Florence, to Bologna, and to Venice, where he studied with ardour the works of the great colourists, and returned by Mantua to Rome in 1623. Returned to Genoa, he was invited by Emmanuel Philibert, of Savoy, Viceroy of Sicily, to his court at Palermo, where he made a long stay. After a residence of more than three years in Italy, where he left a number of remarkable works, especially portraits of rare excellence, Van Dyck returned to Antwerp in 1625, by way of Paris, where he stayed a short time. He arrived in London towards the close of 1627; but disappointed at not receiving the encouragement he had expected under Charles I., he returned to Antwerp, and for six years continued painting numerous works in the Low Countries. The immense reputation which he thus acquired, induced Charles I. to recall him to England, and soon after his arrival in 1632, he was loaded with riches and honours. He received from the king a considerable salary, was knighted on the 5th July, 1632, and appointed Principal Painter to the King. He died at Blackfriars, at the age of forty-two; it is said from the effects of overwork. He was buried in Saint Paul's Church, near the tomb of John of Gaunt.

9. *Lady Elizabeth Woodville invited by Edward IV. to visit him in his Tent* (attributed to).

Bequeathed by the late THOMAS HUTTON, Esq

DYCK, (HERMAN). Living in Munich.

169. *The Last of the Brotherhood.*

Presented by THOMAS BERRY, Esq., LL.D. In Modern Gallery.

EVERDINGEN, (ALBERT VAN); painter and engraver; born at Alkmaar, 1621, died there in November, 1675. *Dutch School.*

His first masters were Roland Savery and Peter Molyn (called Tempestà). Everdingen painted landscapes, animals, and sea pieces, and particularly excelled in representing storms, pine forests and waterfalls. Having been thrown by a tempest on the coast of Norway, during a voyage which he made on the Baltic Sea, he was enabled to make numerous studies, which were of the greatest use to him in the style of which he was the creator. Bakhuysen was his pupil; and he appears to have had much influence on the manner of **Ruysdael**, who evidently copied him intentionally. Albert Everdingen had two brothers, who were also clever painters. Cesar, painter, designer, and architect, born in 1606, died in 1679, was a pupil of Jan van Bronkorst, and painted portraits and historical subjects. John, the second brother, was Cesar's pupil, and painted chiefly subjects of still life. He was by profession a lawyer, and his artistic works are rare. He died in 1656.

D 2

Landscape Study.

2 ft. 1 in. H., 2 ft. 7½ in. w.   On canvas.

A dark mountain torrent, with broken trees lying across.

Presented to the Gallery by ROBERT CLOUSTON, Esq.

FLINCK, (GOVAERT); born at Cleves, in 1614; died, 1660. *Dutch School.*

His father was treasurer of his native town, and destined him for commercial pursuits; but his predilections for art were too strong, and he ultimately devoted himself to it. He was first a scholar of Lambert Jacobs; afterwards entered the school of Rembrandt, and became one of his most distinguished followers. He painted historical subjects and portraits with great success. He received important commissions from the magistrates of Amsterdam for the Stadt House. His style varied from that of his great master, being far behind him in poetic conception and depth of effect; but his works are characterized by truthfulness in composition and colour, which are gradually raising them in the esteem of connoisseurs.

64. Bathsheba's appeal to David.

3 ft. 8 in. H., 5 ft. w.   On canvas.

The painter has here sought to illustrate the 15th, 16th, and 17th verses of first chapter of 1 Kings, which record Bathsheba's appeal to David in favour of her son Solomon :—" And Bathsheba went in unto the king into the chamber; now the king was very old, and Abishag the Shunammite ministered unto the king. And Bathsheba bowed and did obeisance to the king. And the king said to her, What wouldest thou? And she said unto him, My lord, thou swarest by the Lord thy God unto thine handmaid, saying Assuredly Solomon thy son shall reign after me, and he shall sit upon my throne." The aged king leans towards Bathsheba, placing his hand upon the regalia upheld upon a cushion by the Shunammite woman, in assurance of assent to the claim of Solomon's mother. Signed and dated, G. Flinck, f. 1651.

Purchased in London, in 1867.

FONTANA, (LAVINIA); born, 1552; died, 1614. *Bolognese School.*

She was one of a Bolognese family of painters, daughter of Prospero Fontana, an artist of some eminence, who was also her master. She painted many large pictures in the churches of Bologna, and in other places, but obtained more reputation for portraiture than for historical subjects. She painted many portraits in Rome, where she spent the latter portion of her life.

76. The Visit of the Queen of Sheba to Solomon.

10 ft. 7¾ in. w., 8 ft. 5 in. H.

The picture is in reality a portrait group of the Duke of Mantua of the time, with his wife and family, and is most interesting as a representation of the costume of the period, the ladies dresses especially being finished with much elaboration and being of the greatest magnificence; the jewelry alone in the picture would be an interesting study for the antiquary. The drawing on the whole is good, and the colouring excellent. The state is very pure, the picture having only left the palace for which it was painted a few years ago, when it was purchased by H.I.H. Prince Napoleon. It formed part of his collection in the Palais Royale when it was burned by the Communists in 1872, on which occasion a few pictures were saved, and subsequently sold at Christie and Manson's in London, when this one was purchased for the Gallery, 1872.

FRANCIA. [See RAIBOLINI, No. 5.]

FRANCKEN, FRANCK, or VRANCK, (FRANZ); called the Elder, or more commonly, " Old Francks ;" born at Herenthals, or at Antwerp, about 1544; died at Antwerp, 1616. *Flemish School.*

His father, Nicholas Franck (died at Herenthals in 1591), who was but an inferior painter, placed him in the studio of Franz Florio. He was member of the confraternity of Saint Luke in 1566, and deacon of it in 1588 and 1589. The Francks form a numerous family of artists, whose works, spread through all the galleries of Europe, are executed in nearly the same style, and are frequently confounded one with another. The genealogy of the Franck family, for want of sufficient documents, is not established in any certain manner, and their biographers do not agree as to either their precise relationship, or the dates of their births and deaths.

24. *Saint Christopher and the Infant Christ.*

4 in. H., 5¾ in. W. On copper: in oil.

The picture represents, in the foreground, Saint Christopher in the act of raising the Infant Christ to carry him across a river. The saint, according to his legend, is of gigantic stature, using an uprooted palm tree as a staff. A hermit, bearing a torch, stands a little behind, and a group of people, seated on the opposite bank, wait to be carried over. A troop of demons, and a house on fire, in the background, have also reference to the details of his story, which was a very favourite subject among the early painters. See Mrs. Jameson's "Sacred and Legendary Art," vol. ii.

Formerly in the Krüger collection, at Minden.

Deposited in the Gallery by the Trustees of the National Gallery of London.

FYT, (JAN.); born at Antwerp, 1625; died, 1671. *Flemish School.*

One of the most eminent animal painters of his time, distinguished by the fidelity with which he painted from nature, as well living as dead animals. Singularly easy and spirited in touch.

43. *Study of a Wild Boar's Head.*

1 ft. 8½ in. H., 2 ft. 3 in. W.

Evidently painted from the life, and exhibiting great mastery in treating the varied surfaces of hair, teeth, tongue, &c.

Purchased for the Gallery, in Dublin, in 1866.

GAINSBOROUGH, (THOMAS, R.A.) ; born, 1727 ; died, 1788. *British School.*

A native of Suffolk. Developed a genius both for landscape and portrait painting at a remarkably early age, and rapidly rose to the highest popularity and success in the latter branch, retaining his position till his death. Was one of the original members of the Royal Academy. His pictures are distinguished by a facility and masterly simplicity of execution, and an unfailing sentiment of colour that is most delightful; and unlike his great contemporary, Reynolds, he was happy in adopting early in his practice a simple material and method of painting which is equally remarkable for brilliant purity of colour and durability ; his pictures generally retaining all their freshness unimpaired. He is esteemed by many the greatest colourist of the British School.

129. *Portrait of Hugh, Duke of Northumberland,* K.G.; born 1712; died 1786.

2 ft. 5 in. H., 2 ft. W.

Was Lord Lieutenant of Ireland, and as such, distinguished by the interest he took in the charitable and benevolent institutions of Dublin. Oval, with corners filled in, head and shoulders, in crimson dress with ribbon and star of the garter. A fine full-length portrait of His Grace was painted by Reynolds for the Corporation of Dublin, and is now in the Mansion House.

Purchased for the Gallery, in London, 1872.

GENISSON. [Living.] *Flemish School.*

168. *Interior of the Church of St. Jacques, at Antwerp.*

Painted in conjunction with M. Willems.

5 ft. 3 in. H., 4 ft. 2 in. W. On canvas.

Presented to the IRISH INSTITUTION, for the National Gallery of Ireland, by the Earl of CHARLEMONT, 1853.

GHIRLANDAJO (RIDOLFI CORRADI), called ; born at Florence in 1485 ; died in 1560. *Florentine School.*

He was son of Domenico Corradi, called Ghirlandajo from his father who had been a flower or garland maker. Ridolfi's father having died when he was young, he was taken in charge by his uncle, Davide Corradi. He studied under Fra Bartolommeo; and Raphael, when he visited Florence, was so satisfied with his ability as to have desired to enlist him as an assistant in his great works in the Vatican. His works have the stamp of transition of style, from the dry Peruginesque to the more developed style of Raphael and Michael Angelo.

98. *Virgin, Infant Christ, and St. John, in a landscape.*

3 ft. 3¼ in. H., 2 ft. 4 in. W. On panel.

The Virgin, Infant Christ, and St. John, form a group in the foreground of the picture, while the figure of St. Joseph in the

background advancing with an ass, would indicate the preparation for the flight into Egypt. Painted in tempera.

Purchased in 1866 in Paris, at the sale of the Comte de Choiseul's
collection.

GIORGIONE, (GIORGIO BARBARELLI); born, 1477; died, 1511.
Venetian School.

He was born at Trevigi, and showing talent for art when a youth, was
placed as a pupil with **Giovanni Bellini,** somewhat before the time at which
Titian entered his school. He was the first to break away from the somewhat stiff manner of his master, and in his short life carried breadth and
mastery of handling, and rich and harmonious colouring, to its highest
point; he may claim to have been in these qualities more than Bellini,
the real master of Titian. Very few of his oil pictures remain, and his
frescoes have, for the most part, either disappeared, or are much injured.

The figure on the left in the picture No. 100 under the name of
Bellini.

A thoroughly characteristic and powerful piece of painting.

GOZZOLI, BENOZZO DI LESE; born at Florence in 1424; still
living in 1485. *Florentine School.*

He was a pupil of **Fra Giovanni da Fiesole,** (called **Fra Angelico**), with
whom he worked at Orvieto, in 1447, and whose style he imitated in the
paintings which he made from 1450 to 1452, in the churches of Monte-
Falco, a little town of Umbria. He afterwards painted in a less stiff manner at Florence; but it was at the Campo Santo of Pisa that he accomplished his greatest work. He painted there, in fresco, on a wall which
occupies the whole length of the edifice, a series of twenty-four pictures
from the Old Testament—a colossal enterprise, which was commenced in
1469, and terminated in 1485, not finished in two years, as has been pre-
tended. The Pisans erected a tomb to him during his lifetime; it is in
the middle of the Campo Santo, with the date 1478, and bears an epitaph,
which Vasari has preserved.

110. *History of Lucretia.*

1 ft. 3½ in. H., 4 ft. 11 in. W. On panel.

According to the fashion of the very early period of the art to
which this work is to be referred, several incidents are represented in the same picture. It is divided into three compartments: the first containing the Suicide of Lucretia; the second,
the Oath of Brutus over her dead body; and the third, the Ex-
pulsion of the Tarquins. It was formerly customary in Italy to
send wedding presents in chests or boxes painted with suitable
scenes, often by the best masters of the day; and this appears to
be a panel from such a chest. The story of Lucretia was very
frequently chosen as one of the subjects for this species of decoration. This picture has also been attributed to Filippo, and to
Filippino Lippi [see LIPPI.] It possesses something of his silvery
delicacy of colour, and is full of fine dramatic expression. In
good state.

Purchased in Rome, 1856, for the National Gallery of Ireland.

GOSSAERT, (John, called Jan de Mabuse); born at Mabeuge (Mabuse), in Hainault, about 1470; died in Antwerp, in 1532. *Flemish School.*

The exact date of his birth, and the name of his master, are alike unknown. He travelled a good deal; first in England, where his earliest known picture is still extant at Hampton Court—portraits of the three children of Henry VII., dated 1495. He followed Philip de Bourgogne, Ambassador of Maximilian, to the court of Pope Julius II., where he sojourned for upwards of twelve years, copied the remains of ancient art, and the works of the modern painters; and, on his return to the Low Countries, accomplished the revolution in art which had been commenced by Quentin Matsys. He inhabited Utrecht and Middelburgh for a long time, and was much engaged in painting portraits and subjects from history. After the death of the prelate, Philip of Bourgogne, he entered the service of the Marquis de Veere. His pictures possess great interest from the wonderful detail and power of colour; and also as exhibiting, after his sojourn in Italy, the influence of Italian study. The finest work of his perhaps extant, is the well-known "Adoration of the Magi," at Castle Howard, which was obtained by the late Earl of Carlisle from the Orleans collection.

5. *Virgin and Infant Christ.*

11¼ in. h., 9¼ in. w.　On panel.

The Virgin is seated in a niche; the Infant on her lap, springing forward, with outstreched arms, looking upwards; round the arch of the niche is inscribed G e. 3. Mulieris Semen IHS. Serpentis Caput Contrivit. Mabuse has repeated this treatment several times. A signed picture is in Munich. Similar works in the Belvedere at Vienna, and in Madrid.

From the Beaucousin collection. Deposited by the Trustees of National Gallery of England.

GREY, (Charles, r.h.a.).　*British School.*

164. *Glen Isla; in the Highlands of Scotland.*

Presented to the Gallery by Alexander Thom, esq. (In Modern Gallery.)

GUARDI (Francesco); born at Venice in 1712; died in 1793. *Venetian School.*

He was a pupil of Canaletto's, whose style he followed; but his works are distinguishable by a freedom of pencil and of motion superior to other scholars of this master, and in many respects preferable to the laboured conventionalism of Antonio Canal himself, in some of his works.

92. *The Doge's State Barge.*

1 ft. 3½ in. h., 1 ft. 10½ in. w.　On canvas.

The gilded barge is represented in full speed, bearing, presumably, the Doge to his espousal of the Adriatic. The scene is alive with gondolas in motion.

Purchased in London in 1864.

GUERCINO. [See Barbieri.]

HAARLEM (DIRK, THEODORE VAN); born at Haarlem about 1410; died, 1470. *Dutch School.*

Although Van Mander speaks very highly of this painter, as one of the earliest founders of the Dutch School, he makes no mention of his master. Yet his style evidently points to the school of Van Eyck and Memling. Niewenhuys indeed, in describing pictures undoubtedly by him in the collection of the King of Holland, points out the decided similarity of style. His proper name was Stuerbout, and he was called Dirk Von Haarlem from his birth in that town, and Dirk de Louvain from practice of his art there. From the similarity of style, his works at Louvain and elsewhere have been attributed to Memling.

4. *St. Luke sketching the Virgin.*

1 ft. 7½ in. H., 1 ft. 2 in. w. On panel.

The saint, as depicted here, is almost *a da capo* of St. Luke, in the well-known picture by Van Eyck, in the Munich Gallery. The picture, obviously of the time and school, was attributed to Memling; but is probably more correctly attributed to Stuerbout.

Purchased in 1866 at the Choiseul sale in Paris.

HARLOWE, (GEORGE HENRY); born 1787; died 1819. *British School.*

Born in London; a pupil and assistant of Sir Thomas Lawrence, whose style he imitated in his portraits, to which, however, he did not confine himself, having painted historical subjects with great success, the chief of which, "Wolsey receiving the Cardinal's hat," is well known from an excellent engraving. Had he lived, he would doubtless have taken a high place in the British School.

160. *Portrait of Miss Boaden (a singer), sketch.*

1 ft. 1 in. H., 10 in. w. In Modern Gallery.

HARWOOD. [Living.] *British School.*

142. *Portrait of Samuel Lover,* R.H.A. ; born 1797; died 1868.

Painter, Novelist, Musician, and Lyrical Poet.

Purchased for the Gallery, in Dublin, 1872. In Historical and Portrait Gallery.

HAUBER, (WOLFGANG); flourished about 1515 to 1540. *South German School.*

This painter, whose merits may be judged from the present example, which, in the qualities of accurate drawing, high finish, and strong individuality, falls little short of the works of Holbien or Albert Durer, is but little known from his pictures, which are few, although his engravings are known and prized by collectors. He was a pupil of Altdorfer.

15. *Portrait of Anthony Hundertpfundt.*

2 ft. 2 in. H., 1 ft. 6½ in. w. Panel.

A gentleman, in the loose robe of the time, lined with thick black fur, looking to right, dull red sleeves, hands easily clasped; a stone wall back ground in perspective, with the following inscription and signature on tablet :—

Anttai-Hundertpfunt-ist ALLt
51 lav-DA-MAN 1526 WH

Above the wall is seen a blue sky with fleecy clouds. In singularly perfect state for a picture of the time.

Purchased for the Gallery, in London, 1872. From the collection of the Marquis de Blasil.

HAVERTY, (JOSEPH) ; born   ; died   *British School.*

166. *The Blind Piper.*

Presented to the Gallery by WILLIAM SMITH O'BRIEN. (In Modern Gallery.)

HEEM (JOHAN DAVIDSZ DE) ; born at Utrecht, 1600, or according to some, in 1604 ; died at Antwerp, 1674. *Dutch School.*

He was pupil of his father, David de Heem, whose manner he followed, but excelled. He painted fruit, flowers, still life, gold and silver plate, and crystal vases, with a rare perfection. In 1670 he quitted his country, in order to escape the troubles of the war, and settled with his family in Antwerp. He had two sons, Cornelius and John, who painted in his style, but were far inferior to him. Many pictures are known, signed by Cornelius, but very few by John ; because it is said the father retouched them so adroitly, that they passed for works entirely by his own hand. John David de Heem had also for pupils, Abraham Mignon and Henry Schook.

11. *Fruit Piece.*

2 ft. 9½ in. H., 2 ft. 1 in. w. On canvas.

A group of grapes and other fruit suspended from a blue ribbon ; a crucifix, skull, serpent, bread, and wine, on a marble slab. There seems to have been an intention on the part of the painter to symbolize life, death, sin, and salvation. The elements of life, bread and wine ; the skull, with a fly settled upon it, death ; and the crucifix, round which a serpent twines, rising above it, sin and salvation. Signed J. De heem, A.D. 1653.

From the collection of M. Schamps, Ghent. Purchased in London in 1863.

HELST, (B. VANDER), painter ; born at Haerlem in 1613, died in 1670. *Dutch School.*

Little is known of this master, save that he resided constantly at Amsterdam, and was highly distinguished and in good practice there as a portrait painter. His chief work is in the Stadthouse, and may fairly rank with the masterpieces of the world. It represents a company of trained bands, about thirty figures, whole length: the Spanish Ambassador is introduced, and is shaking hands with the chief of the band. It was painted in 1648. Vander Helst also painted subject pictures ; but his great reputation rests upon his portraits. He married at an advanced age, and had one son, who also painted portraits, but with little success.

55. *Portrait of a Man in Black Dress.*

3 ft. 4½ in. H., 2 ft. 9 in. w. On canvas.

Half-length, life-size, of a person of middle age, with moustache, and hair combed down upon his forehead ; looks full out of the picture ; the left hand rests upon the hip, and in the right he holds his hat, which he seems to have just removed from his head. Signed, B. Vanderhelst. 1645.

Purchased in Paris in 1864.

65. *Portrait of an old Lady.*

Oval; 2 ft. 3½ in. H., 1 ft. 11½ in. w.   On panel.

Life size bust of a lady, aged 54, in a black silk dress, with cap and large neck ruff, looking full at the spectator. Signed and dated B. Vander Helst, 1647. From the collection of William Brocas, Esq., R.H.A.

Purchased in Dublin in 1866

HERRERA (FRANCISCO DE), called EL Mozo, or the younger; painter and architect; born in Sevilla, in Spain, 1622 ; died in Madrid, 1685. *Spanish School (of Seville).*

Herrera the younger was the son, and in boyhood the pupil, of Francisco de Herrera, *el viejo*, or the elder, a distinguished artist of the early school of Seville. The severity of his father's character, however, early drove him from his home, and he fled very young to Rome. Here, instead of studying Raffaelle, and the other greater masters, he attended to colouring alone, and devoted himself to architecture, and in particular to the science of perspective. He became celebrated for his graceful and easy representation of still life, game, and meats—the subjects called by the Spanish, *bodegones*—and his fish were considered so excellent, that he was called in Italy, emphatically, *il Spagnuolo de gli pesci*, or "the Spaniard of the Fish," among the painters. Returning to Seville, after his father's death, Herrera *el Mozo* competed with Murillo in more ambitious works, and was in 1660, on the foundation of the Academy of Seville, named Second President, or Director—Murillo being the First President. Passing afterwards to Madrid, he undertook and successfully completed a great work of painting—the Assumption of the B. Virgin, in the cupola of the chapel of Atocha—which gained Herrera the appointment of Painter to the King, Philip IV. Cean Bermudez (vol. ii., p. 283), observes that Herrera's excellence in painting does not go beyond an agreeable style of colouring (in which he is fond of reidish tints), bold contrasts of light and shade, and a certain fire and vigour of composition. He is different from his father in his mode of laying on his colours, but he imitated his style in still life subjects (*bodegoncillos*), and excelled him in his painting of flowers.

HERRERA, [Attributed to].

40. *Sportsmen returned from the Chase.*

4 ft. 10¾ in. H., 6 ft. 8¼ in. w.   On canvas.

Apparently a family group ; figures nearly life size. It is not known with certainty who painted this powerful picture, but it has been attributed to Horrera.

Presented to the Trustees of the National Gallery in London, by ROBERT GOFF, Esq., 1856. Deposited by them in the National Gallery of Ireland, 1857.

HERRING, (J. F. senior); born, 1795; died, 1870. *British School.*

An animal painter of eminence.

A Black Horse Drinking from a Trough.

1 ft. ¾ in. H., 1 ft. 5½ in. w.

Presented to the Gallery by Dr. BARRY. In Modern **Gallery.**

HOGAN, (JOHN) (Sculptor) ; born, 1800 ; died, 1857. *British School.*

A native of Cork, where he acquired considerable proficiency in his art, and gained some reputation ; he, however, was enabled to go to Rome to complete his studies, and there produced original works which won him a high position in his profession.　On his return to Ireland he settled in Dublin, and was much employed, chiefly in portraiture.　His own bent was, however, towards the higher and more imaginative aims of his art, and he excelled both in classical and religious subjects.

130. *Portrait* (marble bust) *of the Most Rev. Dr. Murray, R.C. Archbishop of Dublin.*

Presented to the Gallery by the Rev. CHRISTOPHER BURKE, P.P.　In Historical and Portrait Gallery.

HOGARTH, (WILLIAM) ; born, 1698 ; died, 1764. *British School.*

Born in London, the son of a schoolmaster, he commenced his artistic training in the service of a silversmith, for whom he engraved coats of arms, &c., on plate. ·He afterwards studied drawing from the living model at the academy in St. Martin's-lane, and rapidly developed a genius which places him in an unique position in the British, and entitles him to a high rank amongst the famous of all schools.　He may be said to have invented the method of telling an original story by a series of pictures, and in those of the "Rake's Progress" and the "Marriage à la mode," produced works which in their way have never been approached, whether we consider the original invention displayed, the power with which the story is told, the admirable character of all the figures, the grouping, or the drawing and colour.　It was, however, chiefly by his engravings from these and other works that he was known and famed in his own time, and that he made a good income.　He also excelled in his portraits, some of which will bear comparison with those of any of his contemporaries.　His reputation as a painter is perhaps greater now than at any previous period. He died at his house in Leicester Fields in 1764.

126. *Portrait Group of King George II., his Queen, Caroline, Frederick, Prince of Wales, his Son, afterwards George III., and Daughters, the Princess of Hesse.*

1 ft. 2½ in. w., 1 ft. 7¾ in. H.

This picture is the sketch or design for a larger work, which was never painted.　Hogarth offended the King shortly after making it, by the publication of his print of the "March to Finchley," which his majesty took to be a caricature of his guards, and he never again employed him.

In this sketch, evidently from life, the painter seems to have been influenced by the atmosphere of the court, for there is an elegance and refinement about every touch of it which is not usual in his works, but which recalls the unfinished pictures of Watteau and Pater.　It was formerly in the Willet collection, so famous for its Hogarths, and is engraved by Ryder in "Ireland's Graphic Illustrations."

Purchased for the Gallery in 1874. In Historical and Portrait Gallery.

127. *Portrait of Gustavus Lord Boyne.*

Small full length, of which several repetitions are known. This one was purchased at the Willett sale.

Presented to the Gallery by Mrs. NOSEDA. In Historical and Portrait Gallery.

HONDEKOETER (MELCHIOR); born at Utrecht, 1636; died there, 1695. *Dutch School.*

He was at first a pupil of Gysbert Hondekoeter, his father, a painter of birds. Afterwards, at 17 years of age, he placed himself under the direction of his uncle, J. B. Weenix. From his youth he endeavoured to represent the various species of birds with great accuracy, and particularly hens, cocks, and ducks, in which he was very skilful.

42. *Noah's Ark.*

5 ft. 7½ in. H., 7 ft. 11 in. w.   On canvas.

The picture represents the landing of the various creatures from the ark; in the foreground barn fowl and animals. These are by Hondekoeter; the landscape by J. B. Weenix. [See WEENIX.]

Deposited with the IRISH INSTITUTION, in 1854, for the National Gallery of Ireland, by the Earl of ST. GERMANS, then Lord Lieutenant.

HUYSUM, (JAN VAN); born at Amsterdam in 1682; died in 1749. *Dutch School.*

He was a scholar of his father, Justus Van Huysum, and for some time painted scenes and decorations in conjunction with or in the manner of his father. Ultimately he became distinguished as a flower painter almost unrivalled. He also painted landscapes; but his flower pieces were sought after with avidity, and realized very high prices. There is wonderful precision and beauty of colour in most of his works; while others are scattered in composition, and inharmonious in arrangement. His most distinguished pupil was Margaret Haverman; and it is said that many of her works have been sold for those of her master.

61. *Bouquet of Flowers suspended from the Branch of a Tree.*

2 ft. 2½ in. H., 1 ft. 10 in. w.   On canvas.

This picture was in the collection of Wynne Ellice, Esq. Purchased in London, 1864; an exquisite example, and in perfect condition.

JANSSEN, (CORNELIS J.); born at Amsterdam, in 1590; died in 1665. *Dutch School.*

Some say that Janssen was born in England; at all events, he visited England in 1618, and remained there until 1648. He was distinguished, as a portrait painter, for fidelity, clearness of colour, and great finish. He was much employed in London, where, during the reign of James I., and early in that of Charles I. he held the first place, but after the arrival of

Van Dyck his practice ell off. After his return to Holland he continued to paint portraits, with much success, up to the period of his death. He painted chiefly on panel.

36. *Portrait of a Gentleman.*

2 ft. 2¼ in. H., 1 ft. 10 in. w.

Head and shoulders. A young man with long brown hair, looking out of picture, black dress, one hand visible holding up cloak. Painted with great force and firmness.

Purchased for the Gallery, in Dublin, 1874.

39. *Portrait of a Lady of the Audley Family.*

2 ft. 2½ in. H., 1 ft. 9½ in. w.

The lady is in the dress of the latter part of James I. or early part of Charles I.'s reign : square cut body, lace standing ruff. The face finished with exquisite delicacy, and up to the highest standard of this master's works. One hand only is seen.

Purchased for the Gallery, in London, 1872.

JONES, (THOMAS ALFRED) ; President of the Royal Hibernian Academy.

123. *Portrait of the Right Hon. Henry Grattan;* born, 1750; died, 1820.

Patriot, Statesman, and Orator.

· 3 ft. 7 in.

Copied from the portrait by Ramsay in the possession of the Grattan Family, and presented to the Gallery by the Lady Laura Grattan in 1873.

In Portrait and Historical Gallery.

132. *Portrait of the Right Hon. Sir Maziere Brady, bart., Lord Chancellor of Ireland, &c.;* born, 1796 ; died, 1871.

7 ft. 6½ in. H., 4 ft. 3¾ in. w.

Solicitor-General for Ireland, 1837 ; Attorney-General, 1839 ; Chief Baron of the Exchequer, 1840 ; and three times Lord Chancellor of Ireland—1846, 1853, and 1859. One of the founders and chief benefactors of the National Gallery of Ireland.

Presented to the Gallery by his widow, Lady Brady, in 1874.

In Historical and Portrait Gallery.

JORDAENS, or JORDAANS (JACOB); painter and engraver; born at Antwerp, 20th May, 1593; died in the same city, 18th October, 1678. *Flemish School.*

In 1663 he entered the atelier of Adam van Noort, and was admitted into the Confraternity of Saint Luke, in 1615. He married Catherine von Noort, his master's daughter ; and shortly after his marriage, he and his father-in-law adhered to the Reformed Church. Rubens ever gave him friendly counsels, and engaged him sometimes to carry out his designs from cartoons. He passed all his life in his native town, where he enjoyed a high reputation and a considerable fortune. Endowed with great facility, assiduous at his work, he produced a quantity of remarkable works, which place him among the first painters of his country.

69. *Holy Family.*

4 ft. 11., 3 ft. w. On panel.

The Virgin holds the infant Christ, standing upright, with a string of beads hanging in his hands; Saint John the Baptist looks out at his feet; and Saint Joseph looks over the infant's shoulder.

Presented to the National Gallery of England, in 1838, by the Duke of NORTHUMBERLAND. Deposited by the Trustees.

46. *Theology.*

9 ft. 2 in. 11., 7 ft. 7 in. w.

A female figure seated on a lion, high up in the centre of the picture, supports the Eucharist; the Holy Spirit, in shape of a dove, appears above her head, whilst angels hover around in the clouds. Below sits the infant Christ, with a cross upon his shoulder, seated on a globe, and holding out a burning heart. Saint Jerome, Saint Augustine, Saint Gregory, and Saint Ambrose, the four Fathers of the Church, kneel in various attitudes of adoration. To the left of the picture stand Saints Peter and Paul; on the right Saints Sebastian, Agatha, and Catherine, leaning on the wheel, with the palm of martyrdom in her hand. This picture has also been attributed to Rubens, and it can scarcely be doubted that parts of it are from his hand; for instance, the nude figure of Saint Sebastian, which for flesh painting and drawing is equal to his finest works, and far surpasses the known figures of the same kind by Jordaens. The composition also possesses more dignity than is exhibited in similar subjects by the latter.

Purchased in London, in 1863.

57. *The Supper of Emmaus.*

Our Lord sitting at table with the two disciples; he is in profile, breaking the bread, with the face raised and the eyes turned up; a finely painted head, worthy of Rubens. The disciples in attitudes of astonishment, expressed with all the rough vigour of the master. A typical inn-keeper is pouring wine from a flagon into a glass; a paroquet, which Jordaens often introduced into his pictures, perched on a rod over his head, against an opening in the wall through which the sky is seen. A woman in the background raises a dish from the table, her head seems at some time to have been badly repainted after some injury. On the whole a characteristic picture of the master, only redeemed from boorish coarseness by the refined and elevated expression in the head of Our Lord.

An opportunity is afforded for a very instructive study of the different characteristics of the Flemish and Italian schools, by comparing this picture with that of the same subject, attributed to Titian, on the opposite wall. The contrast between the mode of apprehending and treating the event represented could hardly be greater or more illustrative of the spirit of the two nations. It must be acknowledged, however, that in the one point of the expression of the chief head we find an unexpected superiority in the Flemish master.

LANDSEER, (Sir Edwin, r.a.) ; born, 1802 ; died, 1873. *British School.*

Distinguished for singular precocity of genius, having exhibited his first picture, which in some qualities he never excelled, when little more than fourteen, and gained the rank of Associate of the Royal Academy at the age of twenty-four, and academician at twenty-eight. He continued till his death a prolific exhibitor at the Royal Academy. He was, perhaps, the greatest animal painter that ever lived, for although in some qualities he may have been surpassed by others, yet in his minute knowledge of and insight into animal nature, and the great popular sympathy with animals which his pictures excited, in the intense and varied expression he imparted to them, in the wide range of his subjects, in the thorough knowledge of drawing, and masterly handling of the brush, he is unrivalled, and his place in art is a special one. Perhaps no painter was ever more thoroughly and widely appreciated in his own time by all ranks and classes, and certainly none have enjoyed, in an equal degree, the advantage of reproduction by engraving, very few of his works remaining unengraved, and no artist has had greater justice done to him in reproduction. The engravings of his father, of his brother, Thomas, and of the more famous Samuel Cousins, having done for him all that was possible by that art. He will also be known to posterity as a sculptor, by the crouching lions round the base of the Nelson Column in Trafalgar-square. He was knighted by the Queen in 1850.

139. *A Portrait Group.* *(Members of the Sheridan Family.)*

This painfully interesting picture, painted in 1847, and never finished, represents Mr. Charles Sheridan, grandson of the Right Hon. Richard Brinsley Sheridan, during an illness from which he never recovered. He was in the diplomatic service, was a young man of the highest promise, and died at a villa near Paris, where the picture was painted. He reclines languidly in an invalid chair, with a spaniel on his lap, while a little King Charles dog sleeps by his side. Beside him sits his sister-in-law, Mrs. Thomas Sheridan, with a little girl, her daughter, sitting on her knee, whose sad expression shows that she is conscious that something is amiss ; she has just been called to cease her play, and her mother, who has been reading the paper to the invalid, looks to see if even that may not have fatigued him. The ease and grace of the whole composition is striking, as also the masterly execution, every touch bearing the stamp of having been done from nature. Landseer kept the picture in his own room till his death, and it was purchased for the Gallery at the sale of the works which he left behind him, in 1874.

In Historical and Portrait Gallery.

LANFRANCO, IL CAV. GIOVANNI DI STEFANO ; born at Parma, in 1580, according to Passeri ; in 1581 and 1582 according to other biographers ; died, 29 November, 1647. *Lombard School.*

Lanfranco's parents placed him as a page in the service of Count Scotti, at Plaisance. The Count remarking his happy talent for drawing, sent him to the atelier of Augustino Carracci, then in the service of the Duke Ramiccio, at Ferrara. He made rapid progress, and one of his works was immediately deemed worthy of being placed in the church of Saint Augustin of Plaisance. He studied with ardour the works of Correggio. At the age of twenty he went to Rome, and put himself under the direction of Annibale Carracci, who employed him in his works in the Farnese Gallery. He was much patronized, subsequently, by Paul V., and acquired great reputation by his pictures in different churches, above all by those which he executed in the dome of Santo Andrea della Valle. Called to Naples to paint other domes, he united with Ribera and the other artists of the country against Domenichino. The troubles which broke out in Naples in 1646 sent him back to Rome. He was knighted by Urban VIII., and died the very day that the pictures were uncovered which he had just finished in the tribune of Carlo Catinari. Lanfranco seemed born for colossal enterprizes, and his frescoes were far superior to his oil paintings, particularly to those of moderate size.

72. *The Miracle of the Loaves.*

7 ft. 6 in. H., 14 ft. w. On canvas ; figures in foreground larger than life.

Christ stands in the centre of the picture, pointing to a basket of loaves borne aloft by one of the Disciples. In the foreground variously disposed groups express their wonder. In the middle distance the multitude are grouped on a hill.

67. *The Last Supper.*

7 ft. 6 in. H., 14 ft. w. On canvas ; figures full life size.

Christ, seated in the midst of the Twelve, is in the act of blessing bread. Painted with immense spirit and force, with strong light, and which seems to indicate the influence of Ribera, and therefore places them in the period of his residence at Naples.

These two pictures were formerly in the Fesch collection.—See George's Catalogue.

Purchased in Rome for the National Gallery of Ireland in 1856.

LAWRENCE, (SIR THOMAS, R.A.) ; born, 1769 ; died, 1830. *British School.*

Born at Bristol. His family settled in Bath in 1782, where he studied art under Mr. Hoare, and at the age of thirteen gained the prize of a silver palette from the Society of Arts for a copy in chalk of Raphael's Transfiguration. Settled in London in 1787, where he became acquainted with Sir Joshua Reynolds, and in the same year exhibited several portraits at the Royal Academy, they at once gained him great popularity and practice, which he retained in an almost unprecedented degree until his death in 1830. He was elected associate of the Royal Academy in 1791, and Academician shortly afterwards. In 1792, on the death of Reynolds, he was appointed principal painter in ordinary to the King, and also in succession to him, painter to the Dilettante Society. He was knighted in 1815 after having completed for the King the fine series of full length portraits of the sovereigns, chief statesmen and generals of Europe, which adorn St. George's Hall, Windsor Castle. In 1820 he succeeded West as President of the Royal Academy. His portraits are distinguished by much grace and dignity, which sometimes degenerated into affectation and in his later works his colouring had a glaring and almost meretricious character, which rather injured his reputation. His drawing of the face is almost always admirable.

E

65. Portrait oj Morrough O'Brien, fifth Earl of and Marquis of Thomond; born,   ; died, 1808.

The intimate friend of Burke and Reynolds, he married the niece of the latter.

In Historical and Portrait Gallery.

LELY, (Sir Peter); born 1617; died 1680. *Dutch School.*

Born in Westphalia; he received his art education at Haarlem under Felix Grebber, and came to England upon the death of Vandyck in 1640. He was patronized by King Charles I., and remaining in England through all the vicissitudes of the latter part of his reign and the Commonwealth, became on the Restoration court painter to Charles II., and remained in great fashion and practice until his death. It is in connexion with his paintings of this period, and especially of the beauties of the court, that his name is chiefly known. He began by imitating Vandyck, some of his best pictures rivaling those of the latter, but fell into a much more artificial style, probably due to the influences by which he was surrounded.

136. Portrait of James, first Duke of Ormonde.

The famous statesman who played so prominent a part in the history of Ireland during the reigns of Charles I. and II. Full length, a replica of a portrait at Kilkenny Castle.

Presented to the Gallery by the Earl of Carlisle, when Lord Lieutenant.

LICINO, (Gio. Antonio, called Il Pordenone); born at Pordenone, a city of the Friuli, 1484; died, 1539. *Venetian School.*

He assumed the name of Regillo, it has been said, because of renouncing his family name of Caticello, when wounded in the hand by his brother. He is, however, commonly called Il Pordenone. He studied in his youth the works of Pelligrino at Udine, and subsequently adopted the manner of Giorgione, but following always the bias of his own genius. He painted at Udine and Piacenza, and has left a great many frescoes, in the latter of which he displayed the highest degree of merit. His fancy was rich and vigorous, and he possessed an extraordinary skill in the arts of perspective and foreshortening. He was a rival of Titian; and so great was the hostility between the rival artists of his day in Venice, that he was accustomed for some time even to paint with arms by his side. The emulation between Pordenone and Titian was said to have been most useful to both artists. Licino was highly favoured, and presented with the title of knight by Charles V.; he was afterwards invited to the court of Ercole, the second Duke of Tuscany, where he died, not without suspicion of having been poisoned. Three relatives of the name of Licino were his pupils, and have been much commended.

88. Half-length Portrait of a Count of Ferrara (with a dog.)

3 ft. 7 in. h., 3 ft. 2¼ in. w.   On canvas.

A fine example of the master. Three-quarters length, standing, his left hand resting on a dog's head, the face showing a young man of about twenty; full of interesting character, with a strong Venetian glow of colour.

Purchased in Rome, October, 1856, for the National Gallery of Ireland.

86. *Half-length Portrait of Pellegrini Morosini, wife of Bartolommeo Capello, and mother of the celebrated Bianca Capello.*

3 ft. 2¾ in. H., 2 ft. 7¾ in. w.   On canvas.

Purchased in Venice, December, 1855, by the Government, from the heirs of the Signori Capello.   Deposited in the Gallery by the Trustees of the National Gallery of London, 1857.

LIESBORN (THE MASTER OF).   *Early Westphalian School.*

St. Margaret.

2 ft. 7 in. H., 1 ft. 6½ in. w.   On panel: in distemper.

The saint is seated on a dragon, and holds a chain by which it is bound.   She wears the robes of a queen, and a crown of pearls, in allusion to her name (*Margarita*, a pearl).   The dragon is always introduced in the pictures of this saint, according to a very ancient legend (5th century), which states, that on being imprisoned, as part of her martyrdom, Satan appeared to her in the form of a frightful dragon, to terrify her into apostasy, and swallowed her alive; but that the beast immediately burst asunder, and she come forth unhurt.   In these legends the Dragon is used as a type of Sin ; and the power of faith and innocence to overcome sin is the evident meaning of the allegory.   [See Mrs. Jameson.]

Formerly in the Krüger Collection, at Minden.

Deposited in the Gallery by the Trustees of the National Gallery of London, 1857.

St. Dorothea.

2 ft. 7 in. H., 1 ft. 6½ in. w.   On panel: in distemper.

The saint sits on a flowery bank, in an open landscape, with a wreath of red and white roses on her head, a rose in one hand, and a basket of roses in the other.   These, and three apples, are her particular attributes ; her story being, that while she was led to martyrdom, a young lawyer scoffingly asked her to send him some fruit and flowers from the Paradise of the Heavenly Bridegroom, whose dwelling she had described so well ; and Dorothea promised to do so.   When she received her death-stroke, an angel appeared to the young man with a basket of fresh roses and apples, though it was winter ; and struck by the miracle, he also became a Christian.   [See Mrs. Jameson.]

Formerly in the Krüger Collection, at Minden.

Deposited in the Gallery by the Trustees of the National Gallery of London, 1857.

The two foregoing curious paintings are especially remarkable as representatives of the style of very early German art.   They are the works of one of the first scholars of an unknown Westphalian master, who is recognised only under the title of the Master of Liesborn.   They were taken from an ancient and now disused chapel in Lippstadt.

LIESBORN, (*Early Westphalian School of*).   UNKNOWN MASTER.

E 2

Christ before Pilate.

3 ft. 2¼ in. H., 2 ft. 2 in. w.   On panel; in distemper.

Our Lord wears his crown of thorns, a coarse gray robe, and a cord round his waist, and is barefooted.   He bends forward with an expression of weariness and pain, and does not look towards Pilate as he is pushed before him by the soldiers.   Pilate, wearing furred robes and a golden chain, sits in the judgment chair, and looks at Christ, while he stretches out his hands to the other side that an attendant may pour water on them.   His wife, richly dressed, touches him on the shoulder.

Formerly in the Krüger Collection at Minden.

Deposited in the Gallery by the Trustees of the National Gallery of London, 1857.

Christ carrying the Cross.

1 ft. 5 in. H., 1 ft. w.; arched at the top.   On panel; in oil.

Christ carries his cross, bending under it; an executioner holds a cord by which he is bound, and seems about to strike our Lord with a stick.   Three others also seem to hurry him on.   The group is seen through an arch, or from within the porch of a house; and a landscape, with a town and steeple, appears in the distance.

Formerly in the Krüger Collection at Minden.

Deposited in the Gallery by the Trustees of the National Gallery of London, 1857.

The two foregoing singular specimens of an early form of German Art were found in the Cathedral Church of Liesborn (or Marienfield), and date about the middle of the 16th century.   They are chiefly remarkable as curious specimens of this school.

LIPPI, (FRA FILIPPO); born at Florence about the year 1412, died at Spoleto, October 8, 1469.   *Florentine School.*

Filippo Lippi was left an orphan at the age of two years, and spent his youth in the convent called "Del Carmine," at Florence, where he was formally received at an early age.   His life was full of romantic adventures. When about seventeen years of age, he left the convent to amuse himself in a boat on the sea, and chanced to be seized by Moors, who carried him off as a slave to Barbary.   After many years of captivity, he succeeded in returning to Italy, and he painted in Florence in 1438.   He executed many important works for Cosmo de Medicis, and for the churches and convents of Florence and of Prato.   From the convent of St. Margaret, in the latter town, he carried away Lucrezia Buti, a young girl whom he had seen and admired while painting there; and the fruit of his union with her was his namesake, Filippo the younger, called (to distinguish him among painters from his father) Filippino Lippi.   Filippo the elder worked in the choir of the cathedral, at Spoleto, with Fra Diamante, when he died (it is believed of poison) at the age of 57.

118. St. Mark and St. Augustine.   (School of Fra Filippo Lippi.)

4 ft. 2 in. H., 1 ft. 8½ in. w.   In tempera on wood.

This picture, arched at the top, represents the two saints standing, and is supposed to be a portion of the Barbadori altar-piece, No. 586, in Catalogue of National Gallery of London, with which it was obtained, at Montepulciano.   Purchased in Florence from the Lombardi-Baldi collection, in 1857, by the Trustees of

the London Gallery, and by them deposited in the National
Gallery of Ireland.

LOUTHERBOURG, (PHILIP JAMES, DE) ; born at Strasbourg, *circa*
1740 ; died at Chiswick, near London, in 1812. *French and
English School.*
He was the son of a miniature painter, who ultimately settled in Paris.
According to Bryan, young Loutherbourg was placed under the tuition of
Francesco Casanova, and became a popular painter of battles, sea-pieces,
and landscapes with figures. He subsequently settled in London, where
he was much employed as a scene painter, and eventually became a member of the Royal Academy. His easel pictures were much esteemed, but
the habit of scene-painting seems to have induced a loose style of execution
in direct contrast with his earlier works.

165. *Storm at the entrance of a Mediterranean Port.*
3 ft. 2 in. H., 5 ft. 3 in w.   On canvas.

A wild sea is breaking into a port, evidently one of those in
the south of France ; a vessel struggling against the force of wind
and waves in the middle distance, and in the foreground of rocks,
on which the waves are breaking, the remains of a wrecked
vessel and her crew struggling for escape. Signed and dated,
P. J. de Loutherbourg, 1768.
Formerly in the collection of Lord Palmerston. Purchased in London,
in 1867. In Modern Gallery.

LUCAS, (JOHN) ; died, 1873. *British School.*
Was for many years a portrait painter in great practice in London ; he
was remarkable for the number of times that he was employed to paint
portraits of the great Duke of Wellington, who sat to him frequently, and
is said to have highly approved of his portraits, several of which are
engraved. He had a strong faculty for catching a likeness, but was deficient
in original and distinctively artistic treatment.

143. *Portrait of F. M. Arthur, first Duke of Wellington.*
Original study to waist, for an equestrian portrait ; in cocked
hat, and field-marshal's uniform ; a pleasing likeness. Purchased
for the Gallery at the sale of the artist's pictures, in 1875.
In Historical and Portrait Gallery.

MAAS, (NICHOLAS) ; born, 1632 ; died, 1693. *Dutch School.*
Was a pupil of Rembrandt, and greatly esteemed for his small domestic
scenes, painted with a great force of colour. He seems later to have become
a portrait painter and adopted the somewhat artificial style of Netcher,
and was employed by many of the distinguished personages of his time.

62. *Portrait group representing Frederick William, the
Last Elector of Brandenburgh, known as the
Great Elector, his 1st Wife, Daughter of Frederick
Henry, Prince of Orange, their Son Frederick,
afterwards 1st King of Prussia, and Daughter,
with Attendants, &c.*
An excellent specimen of the painter's later style ; in fine con-
dition, signed and dated.
Purchased for the Gallery, in Paris, 1873.

MABUSE. [See GOSSAERT, Nos. 93 and 95.]

MACHIAVELLI, (ZENOBIO DE) painted about 1473. *Florentine School.*

He is mentioned by Vasari as the only pupil of Benozzo Gozzoli worthy of note; but no details are given of his life. The Cavalier Tommaso Puccini describes two works by Zenobio Machiavelli as formerly existing in a church of Santa Croce, in Fossabonda, a hamlet outside the gates of Pisa. Of these, one, a Coronation of the Virgin, was transported to the Louvre; the other is in the Academy (Istitute delle belle Arti) of Pisa. The picture now in the National Gallery of Ireland was brought over from Italy in 1859 by Mr. Uzielli.

108. *The Madonna enthroned with the Infant Saviour and Saints.*

4 ft. 5 in. H., 4 ft. 11 in. w. In tempera on panel.

The composition consists of six figures, small life-size. In the centre is the Virgin seated on a throne, with the infant Saviour standing on her lap. In her left hand she holds a white rose. On her right stands St. Bernardin of Sienna, holding a medallion, inscribed with the monogram of Christ, and another Saint, probably St. Mark, with a book in his hand, but without any other emblem. On the left of the Virgin is a sainted Bishop, with a crozier, and the border of his cope embroidered with fleurs de lys, St. Louis of Toulouse, and St. Jerome in the habit of a cardinal, with a book and pen in his hand. In the right hand lower corner is written, "Opus Cenobii de Machiavelli." A picture of singular interest, proving this master to have been one of the first of his time. Full of delicacy and refinement of feeling, and the heads beautifully drawn.

Purchased at the Uzielli sale in London in 1861.

MACLISE, (DANIEL, R.A.); born 1811; died 1871. *British School.*

A native of Cork. From a very early age he manifested a strong tendency to art, and although destined for commercial pursuits was allowed to avail himself of such means of study as Cork afforded, the chief one being a collection of casts from the antique sculptures of the Vatican, which had been sent by Pope Pius VII. to King George IV., and by His Majesty presented to the city of Cork. By carefully copying these, and closely observing nature, he soon attained considerable proficiency in drawing in black and white, and got into some practice in taking likenesses with pencil, on a small scale, and book illustrations. At the age of sixteen he was sent to London, and entered the schools of the Royal Academy, where he soon carried off all the prizes that were open to him, and commenced his contributions to its annual exhibitions, which he continued until his death. He rapidly rose to the front rank amongst his contemporaries, and was elected associate of the Academy in 1836, academician in 1840, and upon the death of Sir Charles Eastlake in 1866, was offered the presidency, but declined that high honour. During his whole life he was entirely devoted to his art, and gave an example of the most indefatigable industry. His chief qualities were a great wealth of power in drawing, immense fertility of invention, and unfailing conscientiousness of finish, and accuracy in the study of detail. He was deficient in feeling for colour, and wanted freedom of hand, and breadth of effect. It is an instructive suggestion in connexion with the utility of institutions such as this Gallery, that Maclise owed his successful career to the opportunity for study afforded him by the existence of a collection of casts in his native city, and it is quite open to question whether he might not afterwards have excelled as much in colour as in drawing, had he in his early days, while his eye was being formed, been able to see and copy a few pictures by great colourists, as for instance, by a Titian, a Giorgione, a Palma, a Rubens, or a Rembrandt. He was a spirited etcher, and contributed an interesting series of portraits of contemporary celebrities to Frazer's Magazine, under the nom de plume of Alfred Croquis, under which he also occasionally wrote both in prose and verse.

156. Merry ·Christmas in the Baron's Hall—bringing in the Boar's Head.

12 ft. w., 6 ft. h.

This picture, which was exhibited in the Royal Academy in the season of 1839, gives a very good example both of the merits and the defects of the painter. The interior of an English Baron's has in the olden time towards Christmas evening, it is crowded with figures of various ranks and degrees, each engaged in some appropriate action. On a dais in the background sits the Baron at table, surrounded by his family and guests of rank, while the procession of the boar's head enters by a staircase from above, led by the lord of misrule singing a carol. On the right surrounding a table groaning under its good cheer, is a motley group of retainers and mummers who have formed part of the Christmas pageant. Old Christmas himself about to recruit his strength from a tempting punch bowl. The jester on his hobby horse usefully engaged upon a noble piece of beef. St. George having made truce with the dragon for the nonce, pours wine down his throat ; a pair of conjurers are doing their tricks, one that of the egg and ring, while a young lady who has lent her ring for the occasion, feels her finger with a rueful expression, as though she doubted as to its ever finding its way there again ; a child crowing with delight. On the left of the picture, on the floor, a lively group of pages and waiting maids are playing at hunt the slipper, the hunter being a bashful looking youth who has very little chance with the more daring spirits about him ; in the chimney corner an old dame is telling fortunes from cards ranged on her knees, while a happy couple look over her evidently but little anxious as to the result, &c. The whole picture is full of varied expression, complicated grouping, and original invention.

Purchased for the Gallery, in London, 1872.

MARATTI, or MARATTA, (CARLO) ; painter and engraver ; born at Camerano, in the parish of Ancona, in 1625 ; died at Rome, 15 December, 1713. *Roman School.*

He went to Rome at eleven years of age, and entered the school of Andrea Sacchi, where he remained for nineteen years, copying assiduously the works of Raphael, the Carracci, and the great masters. He returned to his country, and did not revisit Rome until 1650, when he went with Cardinal Albrizio, Governor of Ancona, and tor the first time exhibited a picture in public. He acquired a great reputation in painting Madonnas, and was surnamed *Carluccio delle Madonne.* He was employed by many Popes; had charge of the paintings by Raphael in the Vatican, and was commissioned to restore them, and to retouch in watercolours the frescoes of the Farnesine. Clement XI. made him a Knight of the Order of Christ, and Louis XIV. named him his Painter-in-Ordinary. Few artists enjoyed when living so high a reputation, but posterity has not confirmed the eulogies of his cotemporaries. His pupils were numerous

81. *Europa.*

8 ft. 1 in. H., 13 ft. 11 in. W.   On canvas.   Figures life size.

Europa has just seated herself on the white bull, into which Jupiter has transformed himself, holding a wreath of flowers on his brow. Her companions, who have been engaged in wreathing flowers, look on in pleased surprise. This large picture was probably painted for the hall of some palace.

Purchased in Rome, in 1856, for the National Gallery of Ireland.

MARIESCHI, (JACOPO); born at Venice, 1711; died, 1794.

He was the son of Michele Marieschi, who, as well as Jacopo, painted architectural views in the style of Canaletto. He was instructed by his father in design and perspective, and subsequently became a scholar of Gasparo Diziano. He imitated the style of Canaletto, some think more successfully than Guardi; but the latter had a freer and fuller pencil than either.

101. *View in Venice.*   ⎱
102. *View in Venice.*   ⎰ *Companion pictures.*

1 ft. 3 in. H., 1 ft. 6 in. W.   Both on canvas.

Formerly in the Beauconsin collection. Deposited by the Trustees of the National Gallery, London.

MOLA, (PIETRO FRANCESCO); painter and engraver; born at Coldre, in the diocese of Como, in the Milanese, in 1612, according to Passeri, his cotemporary; died at Rome, 1668. *Bolognese School.*

His father, who was an architect, had him taught the elements of drawing by Prospero Orsi (called the Grotesque), and then placed him in the studio of Giuseppe d'Arpino, whom he left in order to study in Venice the works of the great colourists. On returning to Rome, he painted for a time in Bassano's manner, but afterwards went to Bologna, where he attached himself to the Carracci school, and particularly to Albano, whose style had much influence on him. Mola finally established himself in Rome, where he was much employed and benefited by Innocent X. and Alexander VII. He was made chief of the Academy of Saint Luke; and Louis XIV. invited him to Paris, but he died while preparing for the journey. This artist is often confounded with Giovanni Battista Mola di Francia, who, however, was neither his relation nor even countryman, and whose true name was Mollo or Molli. Pietro Francesco possessed more vigour and less dryness of pencil. In his works the influence of the Venetian school and of the Carracci is evident.

107. *St. Joseph's Dream.*

6 ft. 3¾ in. H., 5 ft. 2½ in. W.   On canvas.

St. Joseph sleeps, seated on steps, in the open air,—a broken column beside him, on the right of the picture,—his head resting upon his left hand. An angel indicates in his dream the land of refuge. The Blessed Virgin close behind, on the left, stoops fondly over the infant Christ, while angels hover around.

Purchased in Rome, October, 1856, for the National Gallery of Ireland.

Landscape, with the Flight into Egypt.

11 in. H., 1 ft. 4 in. W.

Presented by ANTONIO BRADY Esq., London, 1864.

MOLINAER, (Jan.) ; between 1625 and 1660. *Dutch School.*

A painter of the school of Ostade and Brower, chiefly known for his winter open air scenes, skating subjects, &c. Distinguished by an original and delicate humour.

45. *Peasants teaching a Cat and Dog to dance.*

l ft. 9 in. H., 2 ft. 3¾ in. w. Panel.

A group sitting round a cottage table, on the right a young man in profile wearing the buff jerkin of a soldier, holds up a dog by the fore paws, who stands, with a resigned expression of face, on the table. A man in loose cap stands facing us, holding up a cat on its hind legs by the ears, causing it to dance and howl, trying to release its ears with its fore paws ; a woman sits between them, smiling, while a little girl on the left, stands making rough music with two spoons upon the helmet of the young man, which lies on the table ; two other figures complete the group. Painted with great spirit and freedom upon a transparent warm brown ground. The full signature is delicately traced upon the cross member of the table. The whole in an untouched state.

Purchased for the Gallery, in London, 1873.

MOLYN, (Peter, the Elder) ; born at Haarlem, about the year 1600 ; died in 1654, according to Balkema. *Dutch School.*

He was one of the earliest landscape painters ; but he also painted figures well, and with much life and movement. Little is known of his life. He was the father of Peter Molyn, called Tempesta.

8. *The Stadtholder going to the Chase.*

1 ft. 1½ in. H., 1 ft. 10 in. w. On panel.

A Stadtholder and numerous suite, some on horseback, some on foot, are represented issuing from a distant town, in front of a chateau, with dogs and implements of the chase. Although the figures are quaint in costume and delineation, there is great animation in the scene. Signed, P. Molyn, *fecit*, 1625.

Purchased in Paris, 1864.

MOORE, (Christopher, R.H.A.) ; born, 1790 ; died, 1863.

A native of Dublin ; he settled in London about 18 , and for many years practised as a sculptor with great success. He excelled especially in portraiture, and modelled many of the most famous men of his time, his busts being unsurpassed even by those of his contemporary Chantry. He executed some imaginative works.

145. *Portrait* (marble bust) *of the Right Honorable Richard Lalor Shiel ;* born, 1791 ; died, 1851.

Orator, Writer, Politician and Diplomatist.

In Historical and Portrait Gallery.
Presented to the Gallery by the Lord Taunton.

134. *Portrait* (marble bust) *of Thomas Moore ;* born, 1779 ; died, 1852.

The Poet.

Presented to the Gallery by the Earl of Charlemont, K.P.
In Historical and Portrait Gallery.

MORALES, (LUIS, called IL DIVINO) ; born, 1509. *Spanish School.*

A native of Badayos. He devoted his pencil exclusively to subjects of a religious and chiefly ascetic character, the "Ecce Homo," "Flagellation," and "Mater Doloroso," being his favourites, and many times repeated by him. He seldom introduced more than the head and shoulders of the figures represented, but Spain contains a few of his pictures with full figures and life size. He was commonly called Il Divino, probably in consequence of the great devotional feeling which characterizes his works, although it is possible that the extreme beauty of his execution, surpassing that of all his Spanish contemporaries, may have contributed to gain him the title. His best pictures combine in a singular degree almost miscroscopic finish with great force and breadth of colour.

1. *St. Jerome in the Wilderness.*

2 ft. ½ in. H., 1 ft., 6 in. w.   Panel.

Bust ; head almost bald ; he holds a crucifix in his hands which rest upon a skull ; the eyes are raised and streaming with tears, the expression of painful intensity. The colouring deep, rich, and transparent, especially in the flesh shadows. In fine preservation.

Purchased for the Gallery, in London, 1872.

MORONI, (GIOVANNI BATTISTA); native of Albino, Bergamese State ; flourished 1557–1578. *Venetian School.*

He was a scholar of Alessandro Bonvicino (called Il Moretto), and according to Tassi was one of the most assiduous and successful of his pupils. His pictures are, however, not equal to his master, being, in particular, deficient in the graceful expression which distinguishes the works of Il Moretto. He was an excellent colourist. Among his works the most esteemed, at Bergamo, are the Crowning of the Virgin, in the Church of La Trinita ; the Assumption, with the Apostles, in S. Benedetto ; and at the Cappucini, the Dead Christ, in the arms of the Virgin, with several Saints. He was esteemed, as a portrait painter, next to Titian. Bryan mentions a picture by him in the Duke of Sutherland's collection, called Titian's Schoolmaster, as giving a just idea of his powers in portraiture.

105. *Portraits of a Gentleman and his two Children.*

4 ft. 1½ in. H., 3 ft. 2½ in w.   On canvas.

A gentleman in black dress, seated, leaning on a table with his hands on the shoulders of his two children, who stand at his knees dressed in the quaint but brilliant costume of the period. On the table are letters, one evidently addressed to the person represented ; unfortunately the superscription is illegible ; but on the other letter the word Albino is legible ; it was the birthplace of the artist. The sad expression on his face with the protecting action towards the children, together with the plain black dress, suggests the idea that he has lately become a widower.

Purchased in London in 1866.

MOUCHERON, (FREDERICK) ; born at Embden, in 1632 or 1633 ; died at Amsterdam, in 1686. *Dutch School.*

He was a pupil of Asselyn, and went to Paris, where his pictures were much sought after. Helmbrecker painted figures and animals in his landscapes. After many years sojourn in France, he returned to Holland, and settled in Amsterdam, where Adrian Van de Velde and Lingelbach aided him, as Helmbrecker had done. His landscapes are pleasing ; his foliage graceful and breezy; he generally introduced waterfalls and buildings in his scenery. Though inferior to Both his best pictures are highly prized. His son and pupil, Isaac, was a painter and engraver; born in Amsterdam in 1670; he lost his father at sixteen years of age. At twenty-four he visited Italy, and passed many years in painting constantly the environs of Rome and Tivoli. He was received in the academy of Rome, and on account of the accuracy of his drawing and perspective, got the surname of Ordonnance. On his return to Amsterdam, he painted many large landscapes; he also painted figures and animals, but was generally aided in that department by De Wit and Verkolie.

52. *Landscape, with Sheep and Herd.*

3 ft. 8¼ in. h., 3 ft. w. On canvas.

In the foreground of the picture, trees rise high up against the sky; under their shade, some sheep, with a herd; in the middle distance a waterfall, descending from distant mountains.

Purchased at Archdeacon Thorpe's sale at Durham, in 1863.

Italian Landscape, with Muleteers.

1 ft. 4 in. h., 1 ft. 1 in. w. On panel.

An Italian villa crowns a high hill in the centre of the picture, while through an arch below, and to the right, a distant view of country is obtained; a train of muleteers passes along the road in front. This is most probably the work of Isaac Moucheron.

Purchased in London in 1863.

MURILLO (Don Bartolome Estevan); born in Seville in 1618; died in that town on the 3rd of April, 1682. *School of Seville.*

According to Palomino he was born at Pilas, about five leagues from Seville; Cean Bermudez, however, has found on record that he was baptized in the Church of St. Mary Magdalen in Seville, on the 1st of January, 1618. He studied in that city, first in the school of his uncle, Juan del Castillo. In 1643 he went to Madrid, and through the instrumentality of Velazquez, then painter to the king, under whose instruction he placed himself, he had ample opportunity of studying and copying the principal works in the Escurial and other royal residences. Titian, Rubens, Vandyck, Ribera, and Velazquez, were his chosen models. He returned to Seville in 1645. Thenceforth he produced numerous works, which were held in high esteem, and brought him much money, although it is said that he died in narrow circumstances. His best works are said to have been produced from 1670 to 1682. He founded at Seville an Academy of Drawing, which was opened in 1660. Murillo was a most prolific painter, excelling in all works of art, depicting the peasant and the beggar with a happy fidelity, and treating the highest subject with a poetic realism totally distinct from all conventional idealism. His portraits, though not numerous, are faithful and noble in treatment. The Spaniards attribute to him three manners of painting, distinguished as the cold (or silvery), the warm, and the vapoury. But he seems rather to have adopted and applied these manners as proper to the particular subjects, than to have formed them at various periods of his practice. He was summoned to Cadiz in 1681, to execute the paintings for the chief altar of a convent, where, unfortunately he fell from a high scaffold, returned to Seville, where he died.

30. *Portrait of Josua Van Belle.*

4 ft. 1 in. h., 3 ft. 4 in. w. On canvas.

A half length portrait, life size, of a gentleman in a peculiar costume, black doublet, and cloak with a falling neck collar, and white sleeves shown through the slashes of the doublet. He is fair, with long falling hair, looks straight to the spectator, carries his gloves in his left hand, and his hat in his right, falling by his side. A background of curtain and gray silvery sky. There is great relief and simple dignity about the picture. On the back of the original canvas is inscribed in large characters, painted freely, with a brush :—

Josua van Belle

BAR ᴹᴱ ᵀᴴ MVR

LLO

en sevilla año 1670=

This is possibly Josua Van Belle of Rotterdam, whose celebrated collection of pictures was sold there in 1730. *Vide* Gerard Hoet's catalogues of sales in Holland.

Purchased in London in 1866.

33. *The Infant St. John playing with a Lamb.*

2 ft. ½ in. H., 1 ft. 5½ in. w.

The child is represented sitting on the ground caressing the lamb—which looks up at him—with his right hand, the left holds the cross and scroll. Formerly in the collection of Count Besborodko, Chancellor of the Empress Catherine II. of Russia, and was sold with other pictures of the same collection, brought from St. Petersburg to Paris for the purpose, by his descendant Count Koncheleff Besborodko in 1869.

The picture is distinguished by a mellow harmony of tone which recalls Corregio, and is in perfect preservation ; it retains the number of the former collection.

Purchased for the Gallery, in Paris, 1869.

MURPHY, (EDWARD) ; born,   ; died, 1852. *British School.*

A native of Dublin. Studied at the Schools of the Royal Dublin Society, where he distinguished himself. He painted still life chiefly.

161. *Paroquets.*

2 ft. 9½ in. H., 2 ft. ½ in. w.

A white, and a brilliantly coloured paroquet, with a green parrot, perched upon artificial branches ; an admirable piece of colour and handling.

Purchased from the collection of the late Sir Maziere Brady, Bart., in Dublin, 1871. (In Modern Gallery).

MUTTONI, Pietro, (called Pietro della Vecchia); born in Venice, 1605 ; died about 1678, or, as some say, later. *Venetian School.*

He came from the school of Padovanino (see Varotari), but did not resemble him. It has been conjectured that he obtained the surname of Vecchia from his skill in restoring, copying, and exactly imitating old pictures. This habit, however, had the effect (according to Lanzi) of causing him to colour with considerable dulness of light; affording an example to every young artist that he should learn to paint with the full force of colours before he copies similar pictures. Vecchia's style was strong, and perfectly free from mannerism; he drew well, and with extreme facility, preferring to depict youths armed and equipped with plumes, in Giorgione's style, but generally somewhat burlesqued and caricatured, or, at least, not in so easy and quiet a manner—in a manner indeed which, though pleasing in some of his subjects, is, in others, carried to a pitch which has been condemned by critics as absolutely shocking, and even disgusting to men of taste; as in some of his pieces in the Church of Ogni Santi at Venice, at Verona, and in other places. He left several scholars, none of whom, however, followed their master's career.

94. *Timoclea brought before Alexander.*

6 ft. 2 in. H., 7 ft. 10 in.[w. On canvas.

Timoclea was a Theban lady, sister to Theogenes, who was killed at Chæronea. During the siege of Thebes one of Alexander's soldiers offered her violence, when she led him to a well, and, while he believed immense treasures were concealed there, Timoclea threw him into it. Alexander commended her virtue, and forbad his soldiers to hurt the Theban women.* On the right of the picture appears the erect figure of Timoclea, in a state of intense agitation, and on her bosom may be distinguished a spot of blood. She stands addressing Alexander, in a vehement manner, pointing forward with her right hand, the arm stretched out to its full length ; the right foot is also rigidly extended before her, evidently describing the fate to which she had consigned the ruffian soldier. Her figure is seen in profile. In the distance, on the left, is seen a tower in flames, in which the fight still continues, and from the parapet of which some of the combatants are being flung down by those in possession of it. A soldier, unarmed and unhelmeted, but with most of his armour on, seated low on a fragment of architectural ruins, in the centre of the picture, looks up at the excited speaker. Alexander, in a crimson robe, and the attire of a general, seated high on the left, and other soldiers around him, appear to listen to her with awe. Timoclea grasps an infant to her side with the left arm, the right extended as she appeals to the group before her ; a somewhat older child clings to her dress below.

Purchased in Rome in 1856, for the National Gallery of Ireland.

NEER (Aart, Arthus, or Arnould Vander); born at Amsterdam in 1613, or according to some in 1619; died between 1683 and 1691. *Dutch School.*

There is as much difference of opinion as to the place of his birth, as about the date of his birth or death. The name of his master is unknown. He lived for a long time in Amsterdam. He was particularly distinguished for effects of moonlight sunset, and conflagrations. He adorned his pictures

---

* *Vide* Lempriere.

with numerous figures. Adolphe Siret, in his recently published dictionary, thus well describes his powers:—" His moonlights are full of nature. Skies perfectly rendered, rich in arrangement, with truthful colouring and harmonious tones. No painter has so well rendered the poetic profundity of masses of shadow, as well as the varied effects of light and the tranquillity which distinguishes moonlight scenes." His works are much prized, and are to be found in all the principal galleries, as well as in the private collections in Europe.

66. *A Town by a river side on fire.*

1 ft. 10 in. H., 2 ft. 3 in. w.   On canvas.

This is evidently a view of some town in Holland. The portion of the town on fire is on the left of the spectator, the river flowing towards the right. Boats are plying to and fro laden with persons escaping or looking in terror on the conflagration, while in the foreground are a woman with a bundle on her shoulder, and a boy hastening to a boat up the river side.

Purchased at Mr. Farrer's sale in London, in 1866.

NEER, (EGLON HENDRIK VANDER); born at Amsterdam, 1643; died at Duesseldorf in 1703. *Dutch School.*

He was the son of Art, or Arnould Vander Neer, from whom he first received instruction; subsequently he was placed under Jacob Van Loo, a painter of history and portraits at Amsterdam. He went to Paris at twenty years of age, and after his return to Holland married, according to Smith, a lady of large fortune. Indeed, he is reported to have been thrice married, and had large families by his first two wives. His pictures are distinguished by smooth finish and fineness of touch, and are conceived much in the manner of Metzu, Terburg, and Netscher: they are chiefly conversation pieces. He was the master of Adrian Vanderwerf, and his portrait by himself, is placed among the illustrious painters in the Florence Gallery. He was for some time employed by the Elector Palatine at Duesseldorf, where he died. Bryan says, his works are rare, and Smith, in his *Catalogue Raisonné*, quotes several as having brought high prices at public sales.

61. *Going to the Chase.*

1 ft. 10 in. H., 1 ft. 7 in. w.   On copper.

Full length portrait of a gentleman in the full costume of the seventeenth century; he stands in the centre of the picture, with a landscape and sky behind him. In his left hand he holds a riding whip, while with his right he caresses a black greyhound who has sprung upon him. A servant man is engaged coupling a pair of spaniels, and another servant leads up a prancing horse.

O'CONNOR, (JAMES A.); born 1793; died about 1850. *British School.*

A native of Dublin; distinguished himself as a landscape painter early in the present century. Danby, who had studied under him, accompanied him to England about 1819, but O'Connor returned to Dublin from Bristol. He, however, two years later again visited England, where he travelled sketching, about the year 1822; he eventually settled in London, and frequently exhibiting in the Royal Academy till his death. His earlier pictures, painted in Dublin, or amongst the beauties of the County Wicklow, are his best, and considering the poverty of Ireland in good accessible pictures for study, he must be awarded the credit of rare originality and independence of style. His pictures are now highly and increasingly esteemed. An admirable and very interesting series of sketches done during one of his tours in England will be found in the Water-colour Gallery.

163. *A view in the Dargle.*

1 ft. 2 in. ¼ H., 1 ft. 7¾ in. w.

An excellent example of the painter's power of tree drawing and masterly handling of colour.

Purchased for the Gallery, in London, 1873.

158. *Moonlight.*

7 in H., 6½ in. w.

A clear moon, with clouds wildly drifting about it ; a solitary wayfarer is seen in the foreground walking on a road, which forms a perspective in the picture.

Purchased for the Gallery, in London, 1872.

(Both in Modern Gallery.)

ORIZONTE. [See J. F. VAN BLOEMEN, No. 77.]

ORLEY, (BERNHARD VAN) ; born at Brussels, 1471 ; died, 1541. *Flemish School.*

He is also known as Barend Van Brussel, and was born of a noble family of Brussels. He quitted his native country for a long stay at Rome, where he was intimate with Raphael, whose style he adopted. On his return he was named painter to Margaret of Austria, then regent of the Low Countries ; and continued to hold the same position under her successor, Maria of Hungary. He was the master of Michael Van Coxcyen, or Coxcie, with whom he superintended the execution of the tapestries, which Leo X. had made in Belgium after the designs of Raphael. Like Mabuse, he represented the mixed influence of Flemish and Italian art. His earlier works exhibit great earnestness of feeling.

3. *Portrait of a Lady reading.*

1 ft. 7 in. H., 1 ft. 4 in. w. On panel.

A lady, dressed in crimson boddice, with a veil head-dress, is reading an illuminated book. This is evidently a portrait, though from the small vase upon the table it is styled a Magdalen. A picture similar in design, size, and of the same person, is in the National Gallery, London.

Purchased in Paris, 1864.

OSTADE, (ADRIEN VAN) ; born 1610 ; died 1685. *Dutch School.*

A native of Lubeck ; he studied at Haarlem with Brower under F. Hals, and painted for many years with great success ; driven thence by the invasion of the French in 1662, he went to Amsterdam, where he remained in great repute till his death. He confined himself chiefly to very small pictures of peasant life, with a good deal of course humour, very high finish, and fine colour. Great luminous depth in his later pictures.

32. *Boors drinking and singing.*

1 ft. ½ in. H., 1 ft. 8 in. w. Panel.

A group of Boors, men and women, singing boisterously, and in their midst a cat quietly sleeping on the top of a little cask ; full of quaint fun ; the colour very delicate ; in the painter's early manner.

Purchased for the Gallery, in London, 1873.

PADOVANINO, IL. [See VAROTARI, Nos. 17 and 49.

PALMA, (Jacopo); called Il Giovane, or the Younger, to distinguish him from his uncle, Jacopo Palma il Vecchio. Born in 1544 ; died, 1628. *Venetian School.*

Educated at first by his father, Antonio, an inferior painter, Palma *il giovanne* improved himself by studying and copying the works of Titian and the best Venetian masters. At the age of fifteen he was taken by Guido Ubaldo, the Duke of Urbino, to his capital, and afterwards sent by him to Rome, where he resided eight years, and designed much from the antique, copied from M. Angelo and Raphael, and, in particular, studied the paintings of Polidoro. On his return to Venice, he was brought forward by the sculptor, Alexander Vittoria, then an artist of eminence and influence; so that in the course of some years he received orders for a great number of works : so many, indeed, that there is scarcely a church or public building at Venice that does not possess some of his paintings. Lanzi says that, overwhelmed with commissions, he became at last careless in execution; that many of his pictures were said to be almost rough draughts; and that at length he could only be prevailed on to give pieces worthy of his name by allowing him first to fix his own time and price, " in which he was not always discreet." He calls him, " the last of a good age, and the first of a bad."

68. *The Blessed Virgin and the Infant Christ, glorified, surrounded in the clouds by Angels. Three Saints in adoration below.*

7 ft. 6 in. h., 4 ft. 8 in. w. On canvas; arched at the top.

In the upper part of the picture, resting upon the clouds, in glory, the Blessed Virgin is seated, bending forward with the infant Christ upon her knees ; the group surrounded by angels. Below, St. Clara, who is represented holding the pix containing the Blessed Sacrament, and St. George, the patron saint of Venice, with armour, and holding his banner, kneel at the right side ; on the left another saint kneels, clothed in a white robe, over which he wears a crimson chasuble. St. Clara is very often associated with St. George, as a warrior saint; as although she was but a Franciscan nun, it is related that, on one occasion, she showed that she possessed much courage. For an army of Saracens having attacked, and even entered the gates of her convent, Clara caused the sacred vessels containing the Blessed Sacrament to be placed on the altar of the convent chapel, and after praying awhile before the altar, she appeared in the open doorway, in front of her terrified nuns, singing with a clear voice a hymn of praise and trust in God, so that the astonished Moors were seized with a sudden panic and fled. Her body was afterwards laid in the church of St. George, in Assissi. In commemoration of this action she is always represented with the pix in her hand, and is the only female saint to whom it is given. (See Mrs. Jameson's "Sacred and Legendary Art," vol. ii., and the memoir of St. Clara, in the Lives of the Saints.)

Painted for the Sanuda family, in Venice ; mentioned in the life of the artist, and also engraved in Venice.

Purchased in Rome, October, 1856, for the National Gallery of Ireland.

PALMIZANO, (Marco) ; born at Forli, about 1456 ; died about 1537. *Bolognese School.*

Marco Palmizano, or, as the name is variously written, Palmezzano, Palmegiani, was born at Forli, and was accounted one of the best painters of the Romagna. He was a pupil of Melozzo da Forli, and Lanzi speaks in the highest terms of many of his works in Padua, Bassano, Crema, and Vicenza. He describes his early style as being "in common with that of the quattrocentisti, in the extremely simple position of the figures, in the gilt ornaments, in the study of each minute part, as well as in the anatomy, which, in those times, consisted almost wholly in drawing with some skill a St. Sebastian, or some holy anchorite. In his second manner, he was more artificial in his grouping, fuller in his outlines, and greater in his proportions, though at times more free and less varied in his heads." He was also distinguished for his landscape and architecture, as accessories to his sacred groups. He marked his pictures generally as *Marcus Pictor Foroliviensis,* or *Marcus Palmizanus Pictor Foroliviensis, fecit,* with the dates, as in those referred to by Lanzi as being in the possession of Prince Ercolani, 1513 and 1537. Kugler says there are many clever pictures by Marco Palmezzano in the Berlin Gallery. In Rosini is a print of Christ administering the Sacrament to his Disciples (pl. 141) from the picture in the Duomo of Forli; there is also a "Deposition in the Tomb," No. 596, in the National Gallery, London. Zani mentions Filippi Palmeggiani, an eminent painter, supposed to be a son of Marco. His death must have been subsequent to 1537.

117. *The Virgin enthroned.*
7 ft. 2 in. h., 6 ft. 2 in. w. On panel.

In front of an arch of rich architecture, under a canopy, with sky and landscape seen through the arch, a throne is placed, on which the Virgin is seated, with the Infant Christ standing upon her knee; at her feet an angel is seated, who sings, accompanying herself on a lute. St. John the Baptist and St. Lucy stand to the right and left of the throne. It is signed, on a cartel at foot of the picture, "Marcus Palmizanus Pictor Foroliviensis, fecit MDXIII." This is the picture referred to by Lanzi, as having been in possession of Prince Ercolani;—subsequently it was in the Fesch collection.

Purchased at the Rev. Davenport Bromley's sale, in London, 1863.

PANINI, (Giovanni-Paolo); painter; born at Plaisance in 1695 ; died, at Rome, 21st October, 1768. *Roman School.*

He studied architecture and perspective first in his native town. Arrived at Rome, he took lessons from Lucatelli and Benedetto Luti. He endeavoured for some time to imitate the bold style of Salvator Rosa; but abandoned it for one more tame. He excelled in scene painting for theatres. He was a member of the Academy of Rome, and was received into the Academy of Paris, 26th July, 1732.

95. *The Piazza Navona, Rome.* On the occasion of a fête given on the 30th Nov., 1729, by the French Ambassador Cardinal de Polignac, to celebrate the birth of the Dauphin, son of Louis XV. of France.
3 ft. 7 in. h., 8 ft. 1 in. w.

This important historical picture represents with almost photographic accuracy one of those great public festivals for which

Italy was formerly so famous. Temporary temples, columns, fountains, and sculptures of all sizes and kinds and paintings being largely employed, with processions, music, addresses, &c. They usually culminated in a grand display of fireworks, for viewing which on the present occasion it will be seen the whole Piazza is being surrounded with boxes like a theatre, the balconies, windows, and even the house-tops being decorated for the same purpose. The box of the French Ambassador may be recognised by its magnificence, and by the arms of France with which it is decorated, which also appears at intervals upon the ornamental barrier in process of erection round the Piazza. At each end of the enclosed space there are fountains flowing with wine, which is being ladled out to the crowd, who struggle and fight for it.

Between three and four hundred figures may be distinctly counted in this composition, many of them no doubt portraits of distinguished personages of the time. That of the Cardinal Ambassador may be seen in the centre surrounded by a group, to whom he seems to be giving directions, one no doubt being intended for Panini himself, who was intrusted with the whole design and arrangement of the *festa*; and a group in the background represents the young English Princes, Charles Edward and his brother, afterwards Cardinal of York, who were then residing at Rome, with attendants, the chief amongst whom must be English noblemen of high rank, as they, both like the Princes themselves, wear the ribbon of the Garter. The crowd, which shows some curiosity is being kept back from the royal group by one of the custodians of the Piazza, many of whom, and servants in the Cardinal's livery, are doing the honours of the occasion to the privileged spectators. This great work is almost an unique example of the Master, the greater part of whose pictures contain but few figures, and those of quite a subordinate character. It seems strange that a painter capable of producing such figures as abound in this picture, some recalling the grace and easy touch of Lancret or Pater, others the humour and vigour of Hogarth, so full of character, so well grouped, and all so subordinated to the harmony and general effect of the whole, should have spent a large portion of his life multiplying the conventional composition pictures of ruins, which were the fashion of the day, and which are associated with his name. In this instance one may fancy that he was anxious to immortalize the result and triumph of his own skill and labour in a recognised branch of art which had not been disdained by a Leonardo da Vinci or a Michael Angelo; and that so he did his very best. It is interesting to observe from the date which is affixed to the signature, which will be found on a stone in the foreground, that the picture was completed in two years from the date of the event commemorated. It was probably painted for the Ambassador, the fine contemporary engraving by Cochin Fils (which will be found in the Gallery), bearing his arms. There is a replica of the picture in the Louvre, which had belonged to Louis XV. It is less finished than this one, and the figures are fewer, and vary considerably from those in the present picture, which are identical with those in the engraving.

Panini was appointed a member of the Academy of Paris the year following the production of this picture, and it may be assumed in consequence of the reputation acquired there by it.

Purchased for the Gallery in London, 1871.

PARTRIDGE, (JOHN); born,   ; died, 1872.

A portrait painter who practised for many years in London with great success. Was portrait painter in ordinary to the Queen.

140. *Portrait of the Right Hon. Sir Thomas Wyse, K.C.B.*, of the Manor of St. John, Waterford.

2 ft. 11 in. w., 2 ft. 3¾ in. H

Born, 1801; died, 1862. Author, Politician, and Diplomatist.

Was Minister at Athens from 1849 to 1862.

In Historical and Portrait Gallery.

PONTE (JACOPO DA), called IL BASSANO; born at Bassano in 1510; died in the same place, 1592. *Venetian School.*

He was educated first by Francesco da Ponte, his father, and afterwards sent to Venice, to the school of Bonifazio, a master who was so jealous of the secrets of his art being discovered by his pupils, that Jacopo never was able to see him colour, except by watching him secretly through a crevice in the door of his studio. He stayed but a short time in Venice, studying the works of Parmigianino, Titian, and Bonifazio. It has been said that he was a pupil of Titian's, whom, in many pictures, he resembles much in his style. Upon the death of his father, Jacopo returned to his native town, from which no prospects of honour or profit could ever after tempt him ; and during his long career he produced a great number of pictures, which are now spread through all the collections of Europe. At first, he painted mostly historical pieces, but soon abandoned this style for one of less power. He then chose subjects in which he could introduce rural scenes, animals, cottages, familiar objects of all kinds—but particularly (it is said) copper vessels—rich dresses, and all the varied effects of artificial light; and by repeating the representation of the same objects continually, he brought them to the utmost point of perfection; although his works are not altogether free from some errors in perspective and in the symmetry of proportions. Titian, Tintoretto, Paul Veronese, and Annibale Carracci, all praised him highly.

The Departure of Abraham.

2 ft. 9 in. H., 4 ft. 8 in. w. On canvas.

Gen. xii. 4, 5.—"So Abraham went out as the Lord had commanded him, and Lot went with him. Abraham was seventy-five years old when he went forth from Haran. And he took Sarai his wife, and Lot his brother's son, and all the substance which they had gathered, and the souls which they had gotten in Haran, and they went out to go into the land of Canaan."

This picture is engraved by Pietro Monaco.

Purchased in Venice by the Government, in 1854, from the Baron Galvagna. Deposited by the Trustees of the National Gallery of London.

91. *Holy Family (with portrait of a Nobleman and his Son approaching to adore).*

1 ft. 3 in. H., 1 ft. 8 in. w.　On canvas.

This is a votive picture, and the portrait is doubtless that of the donor. The figure of Saint Joseph appears on the left, behind the principal group.

Purchased in Rome, 1856, for the National Gallery of Ireland.

97. *Visit of the Queen of Sheba to Solomon* (3 Kings, x. 2).

5 ft. 6 in. H., 3 ft. 8 in. w.　On canvas.

Purchased in Rome, 1856, for the National Gallery of Ireland.

PONTE (LEANDRO DA), called LEANDRO IL BASSANO; born at Bassano, in 1558; died at Venice, 1623. *Venetian School.*

He was the third son of Jacopo Bassano, and was educated by him. His style was copied from his father's, whose subjects he continually repeated; but his principal reputation was in portrait painting. He finished the works begun by his brother, Francesco, in the Ducal Palace at Venice, and left an immense number of portraits and historical pictures. Leandro was created a Knight of the Order of Saint Mark, by the Doge Grimani, and lived in great splendour at Venice, refusing all the invitations to the Court of the Emperor Rodolph II.

85. *Building of the Tower of Babel.*

4 ft. 6 in. H., 6 ft. 2 in. w.　On canvas.

Many small figures busily engaged in various occupations connected with building—wheeling barrows, sifting, mixing mortar, hewing stone, carrying, fixing scaffolding, &c.

Bequeathed to the National Gallery of London, in 1837, by Lieutenant-Colonel Ollney. Deposited by the Trustees.

Adoration of the Shepherds.

5 ft. H., 7 ft. 7 in. w.

Presented by HENRY WEST, Esq., Q.C.

PORDENONE, IL. [See LICINO, Nos. 51, 53].

POTTER (PAUL); painter and engraver; born at Enkhuysen Holland, in 1625; died at Amsterdam in 1654.

He was the pupil of his father, Peter Potter, a painter of moderate repute, and distinguished himself, at the early age of fifteen, as a painter of animals—a branch of art which he brought to its highest perfection, at least as regards the delineation of cows, sheep, goats, &c. He settled early at the Hague, where he married the daughter of an architect named Balkenend, who is said to have been somewhat dissatisfied with his daughter for marrying a "painter of animals:" yet perhaps his—the architect's—name only survives to posterity as the father-in-law of the gifted Paul! His works were much coveted by the amateurs of the day, and Prince Maurice of Orange particularly frequented his study. In 1652 he went to reside in Amsterdam at the instance of his friend, Burgomaster Tulp. He worked from early morning until evening in the field and in his study, and his assiduity affected a constitution naturally weak; he died in 1654, at the early age of twenty-nine. His works are remarkable for lifelike vigour, for masterly pencil—truthful, yet full and broad; and his landscapes, always subsidiary, are still admirable for luminous truth. Sometimes his manner is dry. His greatest work is said to be the well-known "Young Bull" at the Hague, which he painted at twenty-two years of age. His works have risen enormously in money value, are very rare, and difficult to obtain.

In addition to his finished works in oil, the evidences of his assiduous study of nature are to be found in his etchings, which are highly prized, and his original drawings. Four volumes of the latter are described in Kugler's Hand-book (Dr. Wangen's edition) as being in the Berlin Cabinet of Engravings. The fourth folio volume contains chiefly studies of flowers and plants described as being "admirably drawn with the pen in Indian ink, and slightly washed in water colours. Amongst others, his familiar flowers, we find anemones, asters, poppies, crocuses, May flowers, king-cups, tulips, irises, corn-flowers, and one specimen of fruit—the strawberry." Of the application of these studies the picture now in the National Gallery of Ireland is an important and interesting example.

56. *Head of a Young White Bull with Wreath of Flowers on his Neck.*

2 ft. 6½ in. н., 2 ft. w. On canvas. Oval.

The young animal, life size, looks straight at the spectators, his head slightly turned to the left shoulder; his eyes are life-like, and, with mouth partly open, he seems to breathe. A wreath of flowers, admirably painted, is suspended round his neck. "it is difficult," says Smith in his "Catalogue Raisonne," vol. 5, p. 149, when describing the work—then in the possession of Mr. Peacock—"to decide whether this picture was intended to represent the metamorphosed lover of Europa, a sacrificial offering, or a prize bull of Holland." The probability is that it is a double metamorphosis, or the portrait of a young prize bull as Jupiter in disguise. This picture passed from the possession of Mr. Peacock to that of Mr. Morland, from his collection to that of Mr. T. M. Whitehead, of London, from whom it was acquired in 1868.

29. *Rabbits at the mouth of a Warren.*

(The background attributed to J. Ruysdael.)

1 ft. 2¾ in. н., 1 ft. 6½ in. w. Panel.

Three rabbits are close to a hole which opens into their sub-terranean abode. They seem carefully studied from life, and painted with marvellous skill and accuracy.

A picture called "The Rabbit Warren," by Paul Potter, is mentioned by Smith in his catalogue, and it is possible that this may have been a study for part of it.

Purchased for the Gallery, in London, 1874.

POUSSIN, (Nicholas); born at Andelys (Normandy), June, 1594; died at Rome, 19th November, 1665. *French School.*

He was born at Andelys, in Normandy, of a noble family of Soissons. He learned painting under Quintin Varin, at Andelys. At the age of eighteen he visited Paris, where he prosecuted his studies for a short time under some other masters, and greatly improved himself by drawing from casts and copying prints after Raphael and Giulio Romano. After various vicissitudes, he at length visited Rome in 1624, in his thirtieth year. He lived in the same house with Du Quesnoy, afterwards celebrated under the name of Il Fiammingo: they were of mutual aid to one another in their studies. It was probably owing to his intimacy with Du Quesnoy, that Poussin paid so much attention to the ancient basso-relievo: he modelled some of those works. He also devoted some time to practical anatomy, and he attended the academy of Domenichino, whom he considered the first master in Rome. He had, however, to contend against poverty for a considerable period, until the return to Rome of Cardinal Barberini from his embassy in France and Spain : Poussin had been introduced to him, before his departure from Rome, by the poet Marino, who died shortly afterwards at Naples. This Cardinal, soon after his return, commissioned Poussin to paint two pictures—the " Death of Germanicus " and the " Capture of Jerusalem;" the latter subject he painted twice. From this period he acquired rapidly both fame and fortune. The above pictures were followed by the " Martyrdom of St. Erasmus," the "Plague of Ashdod," the "Seven Sacraments," and others. The last-named works were painted for the Commendatore Del Pozzo, and were, a few years afterwards, repeated by Poussin for M. de Chantelou at Paris. Poussin, after an absence of sixteen years, returned with M. de Chantelou to Paris, in 1640, when he was introduced, by Cardinal Richelieu, to Louis XIII., who wished to retain him in his service; he gave him apartments in the Tuileries, and appointed him his Painter in Ordinary, with a salary of £120 a-year. Poussin, however, wishing to have his wife with him in Paris (he married in 1629), departed in 1642, with permission, for Rome; but as Louis XIII. died shortly afterwards, he never returned to his native country. He continued to increase in wealth and reputation during twenty-three years from this time till his death. He was buried in the church of San Lorenzo, in Lucina.

99. *Phineus and his Followers turned into Stone at the sight of the Gorgon's Head.*

5 ft. 6 in. H., by 8 ft. w.   On canvas.

Andromeda, after her liberation by Perseus, was, according to the promise of Cepheus, her father, given to him in marriage; her uncle, Phineus, however, to whom she had been previously betrothed, opposed the marriage, and, in the contest which ensued, Phineus and his followers were turned by Perseus into stone, as represented in the picture. The scene takes place in the palace of Cepheus during the nuptial feast. Andromeda and her father are seen in the background. Composition of many small figures.

Formerly in the possession of Lord Gwydyr. Presented to the National Gallery, London, in 1837, by Lieut.-General William Thornton. Deposited by the Trustees in the National Gallery of Ireland.

PRUD'HON, (PIERRE) ; born at Cluny, 4th April, 1758 ; died at Paris, 16th February, 1823. *French School.*

He was the thirteenth child of a mason, who died shortly after his birth, and the monks of the neighbouring abbey adopted and educated him. The sight of the pictures which decorated the monastery so excited his imagination, that he early showed an inclination for drawing, which induced the Bishop of Mâcon to send him to the school of painting at Dijon. Here his progress in the art was so rapid that he soon became a successful painter ; and after some years of practice he went to Paris, about 1780, to continue his studies. An interesting anecdote is related of him after his removal to the metropolis. About the year 1783, when competing for the triennial prize founded by the States of Burgundy, being touched by the grief of a rival who was unable to accomplish his task, Prud'hon finished it for him, and the picture obtained the prize; the student, however, confessed to whom the real merit was due, and the judgment in his favour was accordingly reversed. Prud'hon soon afterwards went to Rome, where he studied the works of Raphael, of

Andrea del Sarto, of Leonardo, and Correggio, and copied the Triumph of Glory (the ceiling painted by Pietro da Cortona in the Barberini palace), which he gave to the town of Dijon. Canova vainly tried to retain him in Rome; but he returned to Paris in 1789, where (such was the timidity of his retiring disposition), he lived for some years poor and unknown, making designs for vignettes, and for shopkeepers' cards of address, and painting portraits in miniature; but he was afterwards better appreciated, and was much sought after. He was then employed upon various important public works, as in the Palais de Justice, at St. Cloud, and in the Musée; and he painted, besides, a great number of portraits. He finally received the Cross of the Legion of Honour, and was admitted a member of the Institute of France. He is remarkable for the independence of his style during the period of his celebrity in Paris; never having been influenced by that of David, and the other academic classicists of the time. His paintings have, since his death, acquired a very high and still increasing value.

170. Cupid Chastised.

5 ft. 8 in. ii., 4 ft. 1 in. w.   On canvas.

A young girl in white, her head crowned with lilies (emblematic of her innocence and youth), has seized a little blindfolded Cupid by one wing, and seems to revenge herself by chastising him vigorously. A woody landscape background. This picture, formerly in the Fesch Gallery, is attributed to Prud'hon, but is not authenticated.

Purchased in Rome, October, 1856, for the National Gallery of Ireland.

RAIBOLINI, (GIACOMO FRANCIA, son of FRANCESCO FRANCIA) ; was engaged in painting in 1526 ; died, 1557.

Like his father, the great Francia, whose pupil he was, Giacomo was equally painter and worker in gold, and he also signed himself as a goldworker on his pictures. His paintings were, with very few exceptions, much inferior to those of Francesco Francia; but, though less beautiful, his heads were animated, and his manner soft and free. Some of his Madonna? were more than once copied and engraved by Annibale Carracci.

St. Philip Benozzi.

4 ft. ii., 3 ft. w.   On panel.

The saint stands in a landscape, near some high rocks, holding an open book in one hand, and a lily in the other, the emblems of learning and chastity. Two little angels stand beside him, one holding a cross, and the other the papal tiara, which St. Philip had been pressed to accept, but he fled to the mountain of Montagnate, to escape such a dignity. In the clouds the Blessed Virgin appears with the infant Christ in her arms, who holds out a black robe to the Saint, by which the painter refers to his call to join the Order of the Servi. The landscape opens beyond the wild rocks, and shows a large monastery in the valley. (St Philip Benozzi was a Florentine; he died in the year 1285.)

Purchased in Rome, 1856, for the National Gallery of Ireland.

RAPHAEL, [After.] [See SANZIO, Nos. 8 40 23, 124, 125, 126, 127, 128, 129, 130, 131, 132, 186.]

REMBRANDT, (VAN RYN); born 1606 ; died 1674. *Dutch School.*

This great artist was the son of a miller residing on the banks of the Rhine, between Leyderdorp and Leyden. He studied at Amsterdam, and quickly excelled his masters Zwaanenburg, Lastman, and Pinas, rising to eminence in that city as a portrait painter at an early age. He established an Art School which was soon frequented by the most promising students of the time, and remained at Amsterdam, holding the highest place in his profession until his death in 1674. Although wanting elevation and idealism in his conceptions yet he was an artist in the highest sense of the word; reproducing nature in all her phases with surprising force and intensity, whether his theme were historical, religious, portrait, or landscape, and it is difficult to say whether he excelled most in delicacy of finish or breadth of general effect, in drawing, or in colour. Nor can imagination of a high order be denied to the author of the "Angels Appearing to the Shepherds," or "The Raising of Lazarus" (etchings), or the sunset landscape in the Grosvenor Gallery. His etchings, or engravings (for he invented a method which unites the qualities of both processes) of which he executed a great number, are as highly esteemed as his pictures, and still remain unapproached. During his whole life he must have been a man of marvellous energy and industry, as unlike some of his contemporaries he does not seem ever to have availed himself of the assistance of his pupils, of whom the most distinguished were Bol, Eckhout, Flinck, and Maas.

48. *Head of an Old Man.*

2 ft. ½ in. H., 1 ft. 6 in. w. Panel.

An old man with white beard and red skull-cap, looking down. It has been suggested that it may have been a study for old Tobias blessing his son, the eyes having a blind look, and the expression being appropriate to that act. Signed in the shadow of the background.

Purchased for the Gallery, in London, 1871.

REYNOLDS, (SIR JOSHUA); born at Plympton, in Devonshire, in 1723 ; died in London, 1792. *English School.*

He was the son of a clergyman in Devonshire, and exhibited from a very early period decided propensity for art. His father, naturally with some reluctance, yielded to the bent of his son's disposition, and he was placed under Hudson, the fashionable portrait-painter of his day, but a man of mediocre talents. In a few years Reynolds returned to Devonshire, and practised portrait-painting under favourable auspices, especially through the kindness of Lord Mount Edgecumbe, by whom he was introduced to Captain, afterwards Lord Keppel, who on his appointment to the Mediterranean Station, invited Reynolds to accompany him, and thus facilitated his opportunities of study in the great schools of Italy. He was the most distinguished portrait-painter of the English school—perhaps the founder of its reputation, and one of its most comprehensive thinkers. Had Reynolds been born in the halcyon days of art; in the schools of Florence, Venice, or Rome, where a well ascertained system of colouring obtained, he would doubtless have achieved a position in European art equal to that which he enjoyed at home; but the necessity of forming a system of practice for himself, and some of his experiments towards that end, have tended to the rapid ruin of many of his finest works. Fortunately, however, a considerable number remain intact, such as the Nelly O'Brien, in the possession of Sir Richard Wallace, to attest their original excellence. He was an able writer upon art ; the intimate friend of Johnson, Goldsmith, and the distinguished men of letters of his day, the first President of the Royal Academy, and an artist of whom England may well feel proud. His reputation is greatly on the increase amongst connoisseurs abroad, especially in France.

137. *Portrait of Lord Mount Edgecumbe, Vice-Treasurer of Ireland in* 1768–1772.

(In Historical and Portrait Gallery.)

2 ft. 6 in. H., 2 ft. 1 in. w. On canvas.

The head looks off towards the left; though somewhat faded in colour, no doubt from the disappearance, from whatever cause, of the warm glaze which originally completed the flesh tone—a defect of condition found in many of Reynolds' pictures—it is firm in touch, and on the whole in good preservation. The dress, a blue coat and scarlet waistcoat, with gold lace and buttons, is very rich in colour.

Purchased in London, in 1867.

RIBERA, (JOSEF, or JUSEPE DE), called IL SPAGNOLETTO by the Italians; born at Xativa, near Valencia, in Spain, 12th January, 1588; died at Naples, 1656. *Spanish School; and later, of the Neapolitan School in Italy.*

Ribera, sent to Valencia by his parents to prepare for a career in letters, became in preference a pupil of the celebrated Francisco Ribalta, the head of the Valencian School of Painting. He soon made rapid progress in the art, and was already known as a painter before he left Spain. He did, however, leave the school of Ribalta, and landed, an adventurer, in Italy, where he at once applied himself to draw from the antique statues, and to copy from the works of the great Italian painters; and here it was that amongst his fellow students he first acquired the name of *Il Spagnoletto*—the Spaniard. After copying much after Raphael, and the two Carracci, Ribera became fascinated by the startling and often terrible effect of the light and shade in the works of Michel Angelo Caravaggio, so that he exerted himself with such success as to become for a short time the pupil of this master, who, however, died in 1609, when Ribera was yet but twenty. After this Ribera went to Parma, to study the works of Correggio; but so great was Caravaggio's influence upon his mind, that he could not resist finally adopting the peculiar style of that painter, and many of his works are still mistaken for those of the Italian. Ribera afterwards settled in Naples (then a province of the Spanish throne), where his extraordinary ability almost immediately raised him to the highest eminence. In 1630 he was admitted into the Academy of St. Luke, at Rome; and in the same year he became acquainted with Velasquez, on the visit of the latter to Naples, where Ribera became his host and guide. He died at Naples, in 1656, full of honours, riches, and prosperity.

12. *St. Joseph.*

2 ft. 6 in. H., 2 ft. 1 in. w.

The Saint looks up with wonderful expression, bearing a lily in his hand. It is a replica of a picture in the Collection of Lord Clifden, now at Dover House, London. The execution very spirited.

Purchased in Yorkshire, at the sale of the Carr Collection, in 1862.

RICHMOND, (GEORGE, R.A.)

147. *Portrait of Thomas Moore.* (The Poet.)

(In crayons.)

In Historical and Portrait Gallery

ROBUSTI, (Jacopo), called Il Tintoretto, from his father's profession, that of a dyer; born, at Venice, in 1512 ; died, 31st May, 1594. *Venetian School.*

Il Tintoretto entered the studio of Titian when very young, but soon left it, having already made so much progress, that it has been said that Titian's jealousy was alarmed by the presence of one who promised to be so formidable a rival. He never ceased, however, to preserve a great admiration for his early master's colouring : and he inscribed emphatically on the walls of the poor and inconvenient studio in which he now worked indefatigably, night and day, the words, " The drawing of Michel Angelo, and the colouring of Titian," as the motto of an ambitious artist. Gifted with a prodigious facility of execution, and so disinterested as to give gratuitous aid to his companions, he soon acquired a reputation which was only balanced by those of Titian and Paul Veronese. He was accustomed to take the greatest pains in the study of chiaro scuro, designing his models by lamplight, and making models of wax and chalk; clothing them carefully ; adapting them to little houses of pasteboard ; and supplying small lights through the windows, so as to regulate his own lights and shades. The models he suspended from the ceiling by cords, drawing them from various points of view, in order practically to acquire the science of foreshortening. He also studied anatomy carefully, and obtained a thorough knowledge of the muscles, and of the structure of the human frame. To these studies he united the most fertile imagination, and a genius pronounced by Vasari, one of his severest critics, " the most terrific of which the age could boast." He produced an immense number of works, and was blamed by the critics for painting in *all* manners. Tintoretto's particular merit is in the animation of his figures, it being a recognised opinion that the power of action is best to be studied in his works. He aimed rather at liveliness than grace, and drew his heads and attitudes from observation of the spirited population of his native Venice. There his pictures are, of course, numerous; and there we may learn that Tintoretto often wrought with a degree of finish equal to that of a miniature painter, though most of his works out of Venice are of a totally different character of execution. He left a son, Domenico Robusti, who was a good painter, and resembled his father in style, but fell into mannerism as he grew older. Jacopo's daughter, Marietta, was so excellent a portrait painter, that both the Emperor Maximilian and Philip II. of Spain invited her to visit their courts; but her father could not consent to part with her. She died not long afterwards, while quite young. Paoli Franceschi, Odoardo Fialetti, Martin de Vos, of Antwerp (who often painted the landscapes in his pictures), &c., were Tintoretto's chief pupils.

90. *Portrait of a nobleman in black dress.*

3 ft. 9½ in. h., 2 ft. 9½ in. w. On canvas.

This portrait evidently represents some person of distinction, who wears a loose black silk robe, with deep fur collar ; he leans upon a table, and looks out upon the spectator. Inscribed, "1555. Ætatis 29."

Purchased in London in 1866.

ROMANO, Giulio. [See Pippi, and see Sanzio, No. 40.]

ROSA, (Salvator); painter, engraver, poet, and musician ; born at the village of La Renella, near Naples, 20th June, 1615; died, at Rome, 15th March, 1673. *Neapolitan School.*

Paolo Greco, one of his uncles, gave Salvator his first lessons in drawing; then he entered the school of Francesco Fracanzano, his brother-in-law, and Ribera's pupil. At seventeen, Salvator, having lost his father, and being without any resources, painted a number of sea-pieces, landscapes, and small historical compositions, which were sold in the public places at very low prices. Lanfranco, astonished at the vigour of these pictures, bought several of them, and encouraged the young artist, who frequented the studio of Ribera, and afterwards that of Aniello Falcono (Ribera's disciple), whose battle pieces he copied, and whose manner he sought to imitate. He remained nearly three years with Falcone, living in great poverty, and then went to Rome, where he fell sick, and so returned to Naples; but in Naples he still found little occupation. After about two years he went again to Rome, and obtained, by the help of one of his countrymen, some employment from the Cardinal Brancacci, at Viterbo, of which place the Cardinal was then bishop. In the end of 1646, Salvator went back to Naples; and in 1647, when the insurrection of Mase Aniello against the Spaniards broke out, he entered the "Company of Death," which was commanded by his friend and master, Falcone. After the defeat of Mase Aniello, Salvator and Falcone fled to Rome, to avoid the rage of the viceroy, and Rosa remained there, painting a great many works, which were much admired. After four years the Grand Duke of Tuscany invited him to his court. He was received there with the highest favour, and he remained at Florence nine years, dividing his time between poetry, painting, and music. Once again, however, he returned to Rome, where he settled finally, and received very large prices for his works, which now became very numerous. Rosa was the most distinguished landscape painter of his century. He is original in his style and choice of subjects; generally preferring wild and broken rocks, savage deserts, torn and blasted trees, and ruins, with cheerless or stormy skies; and the figures introduced are almost always those of shepherds, mariners, or banditti; though sometimes he represented the scene as that of some religious event, such as the Baptism in the Jordan. He also painted historical subjects on a large scale; some of them finely executed—such as the Conspiracy of Catiline, in the possession of the Martelli family in Rome, mentioned by Bottari as one of his best works. In his battles as well as his landscapes he displayed a truly remarkable vigour and energy. He died in Rome, and was buried in the Church degli Angeli, where his portrait and eulogy were placed. His principal pupils and imitators are Marzio Maturzio, N. Vaccaro, Scipio Compagno, Bartolomeo Torregiano, and G. Ghisolfi.

96. Landscape.—The Baptism of Christ in the Jordan.

4 ft. 10 in. H., 7 ft. 3 in. W. On canvas.

(Attributed to).

Purchased in Rome, October, 1856, for the National Gallery of Ireland.

63. St. John in the Wilderness. (After Titian.)

5 ft. 4 in. H., 4 ft. 2 in. W. On canvas.

St. John stands in a wild landscape, with outstretched arm; to his left a waterfall, and at his foot a lamb. This picture was brought from Italy by Greffiers Fagel, by whom it was sold in 1742, to the Heckering family.

Purchased at Archdeacon Thorpe's sale, at Durham, in 1863.

RUBENS, (Peter Paul); born at Siegen, 29th June, 1577; died at Antwerp, 30th May, 1640. *Flemish School.*

Peter Paul Rubens was the son of Johann Rubens, a doctor of laws in Antwerp, who died when Rubens was a boy of eleven years old. He was at first when a boy in the service of Marguerite de Ligne, widow of Count Philip of Lalaing, as a page; but he early persuaded his mother to place

him in the studio of Adam van Noort, which he soon afterwards left for
that of the distinguished master, Otto van Veen, commonly called Otto
Venius. In 1598 Rubens became Free Master of the Academy of St. Luke,
and in 1600 he started for Italy by way of France, where he fixed himself
in Venice, to study the great works of Titian and Paolo Veronese. Here
he was introduced to Vincent Gonzaga, the Duke of Mantua, who prevailed on him to take service as court painter; and in Mantua Rubens
remained eight years, making frequent visits, however, to Venice and to
Rome. In 1608 the Duke of Mantua sent him to Madrid, charged with a
diplomatic mission to the King of Spain, Philip III.; and Rubens was
received there with distinction, both as artist and ambassador. In Madrid,
he painted many portraits, as well as several copies after the magnificent
works of Titian which adorn that capital. On his return to Mantua he
obtained leave to go for a space to Rome, where he painted the best works
in his first manner; afterwards he visited Florence, Bologna, Venice,
Milan, and Genoa, studying all the masters there, and painting a great
number of pictures in every style. The illness and death of his mother
just then recalled him to his own country, and he reached Antwerp in
1609. Here the Archduke Albert and the Infanta Isabella succeeded in
retaining him, testifying their sense of the great fame he had by this time
acquired by appointing him Court Chamberlain, with a considerable pension. He accordingly settled in Antwerp, where he always lived in a
magnificent style. About 1609, Rubens married Isabella Brandt, the
daughter of the Secretary of the city of Antwerp. She died in 1626,
leaving two sons. In 1621, Rubens was called to Paris, to undertake, in
the Luxembourg, the series of vast pictures, now in the Louvre, commemorative of the principal events in the history of Mary of Medicis, the
mother of Louis XIII. The great painter accordingly proceeded to Paris,
where he made sketches for these works; and returning to Antwerp, he
completed the pictures themselves in four years, with the assistance of an
able staff of pupils. Subsequently to this time Rubens was employed, as
ambassador, in several important political negotiations—for which his
singular ability and the manly tone of his mind eminently qualified him—
in 1628 at Madrid, and afterwards at Paris, and in London. Having succeeded in arranging peace between Philip IV. of Spain and Charles I. of
England, he was, in 1629, created a Privy Councillor at Brussels, and a
knight in London, besides receiving great gifts from both monarchs. In
1630 Rubens married again, in Antwerp: his second wife was Helene
Fourment, by whom he had three daughters and two sons. After 1635,
frequent attacks of the gout caused Rubens finally to retire from court
life, and to devote himself exclusively to his art; and after this period he
gave up also the habit of painting very large subjects, and worked almost
exclusively at small-sized pictures. The great characteristic of Rubens'
genius (says the able compiler of the Louvre Catalogue) is force, motion,
passion—carried to the highest point of artistic perfection. He is never
weak, never hesitating: his drawing is always skilful, rapid, strongly
marked; his colouring brilliant to a degree; his attitudes energetic, even
to an extreme. Rubens had little of the finer taste, the delicate sensi-
bility, the religious feeling of the Italian and Spanish schools; but he
possessed a richness of invention that was quite inexhaustible, and a hand
to which the most prodigious difficulties seemed only an easy play. Rubens
left many great scholars and imitators, among whom the principal were
Anton Van Dyck, Jakob Jordaens, David Teniers the younger, &c.; and
his imitators are innumerable.

2. *Vision of Saint Ignatius Loyola.   Sketch.*

2 ft. 1 in. H., 1 ft. 10 in. w.   On panel.

Evidently a design for the altar-piece of some Jesuit Church.
To the left of the foreground kneels the Saint with an open
book; while two infant angels bear a tablet with the motto of the

order, " Ad majorem Dei gloriam," inscribed, before which three others kneel. On an upper or middle plane the Saviour, with only a garment of white falling from his figure, as if risen from the grave, leans with the palm of martyrdom over his Mother, who kneels before him, and from whom an angel withdraws her mantle. Christ is followed by a procession of saints and martyrs. King David with his lyre, and other figures are introduced, as if to signify the fulfilment of the Law and the Prophets. From above angels descend, bearing a crown and a banner inscribed—" Mater dolorosa lætari, Allelujah."

This sketch is attributed to Rubens ; and, indeed, on the back of the panel is inscribed "Rubbens." In general composition it is quite in Rubens' manner, while in other respects it resembles the pencil of Vandyke.

Purchased at the sale of the Carr Collection, in Yorkshire, in 1863.

51. *Saint Francis receiving the Stigmata.*

5 ft. 11¾ in. H., 3 ft. ½ in. w.

This picture doubtless formed one of the wings of a tryptich altar-piece, the centre subject of which is missing ; the other wing representing St. Dominick with the traditional dog, being in the collection of the Marquis of Bristol. This is remarkable for its sober gray tones of colour, not generally characteristic of the master, but his hand is unmistakeably apparent in every stroke of the brush, the execution being of the most energetic and spirited character. The Saint is represented apparently in the act of receiving the stigmata, and the ecstacy of the moment seems to have driven all the blood from his face and hands. The type is coarse and commonplace.

Purchased for the Gallery, in London, 1871.

38. *Saint Peter finding the piece of Tribute Money in the fish.*

6 ft. 6½ in. H., 7 ft. 2 in. w.

A group of six men and one woman upon the sea-shore. St. Peter having apparently just landed from a boat, has cut open the fish which he supports with his left hand, while with his right he holds up the piece of money that he has just taken out from it, and examines it attentively, while the other disciples also look with excited and surprised expressions. A young woman with a tub of fish on her head looks over his shoulder. One of the disciples is kneeling in the foreground, his back turned to us, holding a rope in his hand, which is attached to the boat. With the exceptions mentioned below, this picture is a reproduction of one painted in a series for the chapel of the Fishmonger's Guild in the church of Notre Dame at Malines. The chief difference being the kneeling figure, which is absent in that picture, the latter also includes the complete outline of the woman. A contemporary engraving of the present picture by N. Lauwers exists, and is alluded to in Smith's Catalogue, supplement, page 255. It is doubtless from the studio of Rubens, as no pupil would have dared to make so striking an alteration, although probably great part is the work of his assistants filling in his outlines, but a few spirited finishing touches are at least recognizable as from his own hand. Such being the method upon which, as we know from his own letters, much of the work which left his studio was accomplished.

Formerly in the Desenfans Collection.
Purchased for the Gallery, in London, 1872.

RUBENS, [After].

154. *Judgment of Paris.*

4 ft. 9 in. H., 6 ft. 1 in. w. On canvas.

At the nuptials of Thetis and Peleus an apple was thrown among the guests by Discord, to be given to the most beautiful ; Juno, Minerva, and Venus were competitors for the prize, and Paris, the son of Priam, was ordered by Jupiter to decide the contest. Paris decided in favour of Venus, and his decision was the cause of all the consequent misfortunes of Troy. Discord is seen already hovering in the clouds above, spreading fire and pestilence around.

This copy of the celebrated picture, formerly in the Orleans collection, now in the National Gallery, London, is attributed to Thomas Stothard, R.A. Many copies of it exist ; one of which is in the Louvre. It is engraved by J. Couché and Dambrin for the *Galerie du Palais Royal.*

Presented by the late WILLIAM LECKY BROWNE, Esq.

(In Modern Gallery.)

RUYSDAEL, or RUISDAEL, (JAKOB) ; painter and engraver ; born at Haarlem, about 1630 ; died in the same town, 16th November, 1681. *Dutch School.*

Much uncertainty prevails as to the date of this distinguished painter's birth ; Waagen gives it as 1625. The name of his master is equally unknown, but he is supposed to have studied under his elder brother, Solomon Ruysdael. It is stated that his father was a maker of frames in ebony wood then much sought after, and that he was sufficiently independent to bring up Jacob as a medical doctor. His true vocation was that of art ; and he is unique as a landscape painter, many of his works being conceived with truly poetic feeling. He was varied in his style ; painting, sometimes, the flat scenery, the sedgy pools, the windmills and roads about Haarlem. Forest scenes, waterfalls, and the sea in commotion were favourite subjects of his pencil. A Van de Velde, Berchem, Philipps, Wouwermann, and Lingelbach illustrated his landscapes with figures ; but his greatest fame will rest on works imbued with poetic feeling independent of extraneous aid, such as the *Jewish Cemetery*, in the Dresden Gallery, or the *Storm*, a sea-piece, in Lord Lansdowne's collection.

53. *The Windmill.*

3 ft. 4 in. H., 4 ft. 3 in. w.   On canvas.

A long winding road, with water at either side, leads to a windmill and miller's residence. The mill rises up against the sky, which is massed with rain-clouds, and the whole scene is indicative of rain passing off. The road and foreground are brown and dark, but much relief is given by the water, and the reflection of the mill and trees. The tone very fine, and the truth of atmospheric effect in dull cloudy weather, especially admirable. It is in excellent condition. The work is signed J. R., 1663. It belonged to the late Bishop of Ely.

Purchased in London in 1864.

37. *A Woody Landscape.*

2 ft. H., 2 ft. 6 in. w.

It is thus described in Smith's Catalogue, Part 6, Page 62.

"A mountainous and well-wooded landscape, divided by a winding road on the left, on which is a man carrying a pack on his back, led by a dog, and beyond him are seen a man and a boy approaching. A pond of water covers the right, on which are three swans; the view is bounded on the side by a lofty hill well clothed with trees, whose dark umbrageous foliage is strikingly relieved by a brilliant mass of fleecy clouds."

A fine example of the master's deeper toned and more elaborately finished manner. The mass of white cloud rising above the trees is especially admirable. Signed with the full signature and dated.

Formerly in the Collection of Mr. W. Beckford at Fonthill Abbey.

Purchased for the Gallery, in London, 1873.

RUYSDAEL, (SOLOMON VAN) ; born, 1616 ; died, 1670. *Dutch School.*

Was an elder brother (by twenty years) of Jacob Ruysdael. Believed to have been a pupil of **Van Goyen**, whose peculiar style he imitated, and for whose work his pictures arc often taken. He possessed some admirable qualities, notably a strong feeling for atmospheric effect and aerial perspective.

27. *View of the town of Alkmaar in Holland, with the river frozen and figures skating, &c.*

This town is made famous by the heroic and successful resistance of its inhabitants to the Spaniards during the Dutch War of Independence. An excellent specimen of the painter's style, and well exemplifies the qualities mentioned above. Signed with initials.

Purchased for the Gallery, in Paris, 1873

SANZIO (RAFFAELLO, RAPHAEL); commonly called THE DIVINE; painter and architect; born at Urbino, on Good Friday, 28th March,`1483 ; died at Rome, on Good Friday, 6th April, 1520. *Roman School.*

The true family name of Raphael* was De Santi or Santo, but his name has always been spelled Sanzio since his time. He was the son of **Giovanni Santi**, from whom he first learned the rudiments of drawing; for Raphael was the fifth painter in his family in a direct line. Giovanni, however, died, when his son was only in his twelfth year, in 1494. Raphael is supposed to have had early lessons from **Timoteo della Vite**, and from **Luca Signorelli**, who were both engaged in the churches of Urbino, in 1494 and 1495; but at the end of 1495, or beginning of 1496, he finally placed himself under the direction of **Pietro Vanucci**, called **Perugino**, one of the most celebrated artists of the time at Perugia. Here he soon surpassed all his fellow-students. In 1500, Perugino having gone to Florence, Raphael left him, and went to Città di Castello, where he painted many original pictures, and where, in 1504, he finished the celebrated *Sposalizio*, or Marriage of the Blessed Virgin, now at Milan. After this he spent some time at Urbino and at Sienna, and then proceeded to Florence, where his study of the works of **Masaccio**, and his intimacy with **Fra Bartolommeo**, produced a marked effect on the bent of his genius. Here he began really to study colour, as well as the art of drapery in painting. During the two following years he divided his time between Perugia and Florence; and it was at this period that took place the singular connexion of friendship between him and the illustrious painter of Bologna, **Francesco Raibolini**, called Il Francia, of which so interesting an account is to be found in the various lives of Raphael. In 1508 he went to Rome, when he was presented to the Pope, Julius II., by his relative the distinguished architect, Bramante. His first great fresco, at the Vatican, was the *Dispute of the Blessed Sacrament;* a work which at once placed him at the head of all the artists then known in Rome; and this absolute pre-eminence Raphael has ever since been allowed by the world, with the solitary exception of Michel Angelo Buonarotti, whose greater power, though never allied with Raphael's delicacy of taste and sweetness of imagination, has gained for him the highest crown of all. It would be out of place here to recount, or even to name, the astonishing succession of magnificent *chefs d'œuvre* of art which Raphael was destined to accomplish in so short a life; nor is it possible to sketch here, with the minuteness which its interest deserves, that life itself. Memoirs of Raphael, long and short, are to be found in almost all the works which treat of the history of painting. [See, particularly, Quatremere de Quincy's Memoir, translated for Bohn's Library (London, 1846); see also Vasari and Lanzi, whose Lives of the Painters are translated in Bohn's series; and see Kugler's Schools of Painting in Italy, translated by Sir C. Eastlake (London, 1851), in which are to be found illustrations and memoranda of all the celebrated Madonnas of Raphael, as well as of his extraordinary frescoes at the Vatican; see, above all, Raphael D'Urbin, by J. D. Passavant]. He was the chief of what has been called the Roman School, a school famous for having produced, according to Vasari, fifty painters, *all good and able.* Among these the most remarkable were the celebrated **Giulio Romano** (see **Pippi**)—the copyist, after Raphael, of the specimen, No. 40, in the present collection—**Polidoro, Pierino del Vago, Andrea Sabatini, Giovanni da Udine,** &c. "The destiny of Raffaello," justly remarks the editor of the Louvre Catalogue, "is unique in the annals of painting. In a few years he exhausted the favours of fortune; his premature death was a mourning affliction to the art itself; and posterity, for once just, hastened to make his very name divine. If he proved

* There is much difference as to the writing of Raphael's name. He himself wrote Raphael, and sometimes Raphaelo; the modern Italian is Raffaelle or Raffaello, but in English Raphael seems more correct, and is the true writing of the ancient Hebrew name.

himself worthy of this apotheosis, it was not that he united in his works, as has often been erroneously said, the different qualities which shine with so great a brilliancy in those of Leonardo da Vinci, Titian, Michel Angelo, and Correggio; it was not, in a word, because he was the most accurate and the most scientific of all painters; but it was because he alone was always elevated without effort, human without triviality, graceful without affectation, full of passion without exaggeration; it was because his simplest and his most gigantic compositions bear alike the impress of a spontaneous creation, full of life, grandeur, and beauty."

SANZIO, (RAFFAELLO); [after].

The Transfiguration.

13 ft. 2 in. H., 9 ft. w.   On canvas.

This full-sized copy is attributed to Raphael Mengs. It was purchased by the Earl of Bristol in Rome more than one hundred years ago. It is in some parts faded in colour, but, on the whole, is sufficiently harmonious, and is a truthful copy of the great original in the Vatican.

Purchased in London in 1864.

70. St. Cecilia.

7 ft. 7½ in. H., 4 ft. 9 in. w.   On canvas.

The saint in the middle of the picture with eyes upturned listens to the heavenly song of the angels. A small organ almost falls from her hands, as she seems wrapt in ecstasy. At her feet are musical instruments scattered and broken, as betokening the comparative worthlessness of all earthly things. To the right of St. Cecilia stands St. Paul resting on his sword ; behind him St. John the Evangelist ; to the immediate left behind is St. Augustine, one of the Fathers of the Church, and in front Mary Magdalene, with her vase of perfumes in her left hand.

This copy, in the finest preservation, was painted by Domenichino from the original painted by Raphael for the chapel of St. Cecilia, in the church of St. Giovanni in Monte, near Bologna. The original was on panel, but being brought to Paris, it was then transferred to canvas ; it is now in the Pinacothek at Bologna. Passavant refers to this copy as being in the possession of Bozzotti, a goldsmith in Milan, from whom it was purchased by the late Viscount Powerscourt in 1836 ; it had been in the collection of the Count Serbelloni.

Presented in 1866 by the Viscount Powerscourt, K.P.

171. Peter and John at the beautiful Gate—Cartoon.

12 ft. 4 in. H., 17 ft. 9 in. w.

172. Elymas the Sorcerer struck with Blindness— Cartoon.

12 ft. 4 in. H., 14 ft. 11 in. w.

These cartoons—full-sized copies of those by Raphael in the series at Hampton Court, are supposed to have been executed by Giulio Romano. They were found by Sir Joshua Reynolds, during his tour in the Low Countries, at some town where they had lain from the time they had been used as models for tapestry.

G

They remained in Sir Joshua's possession until his death, and were so highly esteemed that Holloway, the engraver, is said to have finished his plates after them. They became, by purchase, the property of —— Nicolay, Esq., who proposed to present them to Stewart Blacker, Esq., for a National Gallery in Ireland. Subsequent to his death his intention was fulfilled by his widow, who presented them in trust to Mr. Blacker, until a suitable gallery should be established.

The School of Athens ; drawing in red chalk.

2 ft. 9 in. H., 4 ft. w.

This drawing—most carefully executed—bears the following inscription :—

"Sanctissimo spirito del mio benefattore, altissimo Monsignore Camillo Massimi.

" Gio. Cesre. Maj., Dona, A.D. 1650.

It was formerly the property of the late Sir Thomas Wyse, and is supposed to have been brought from Italy by a member of the Napoleon family.

Purchased in Waterford, in 1860.

112. Large Photograph from the original picture, called the Madonna de San Sisto, in the Modern Gallery.

In the Intermediate (new) Gallery.

SARTO, (ANDREA DEL). [See VANNUCCHI, Nos. 1, 10, 160, and 160a.]

111. Adoration of the Shepherds.

1 ft. 1 in. H., 10 in. w.

From the Beaucousin collection. Deposited by the Trustees of the National Gallery of London.

SASSOFERATO (GIOVANNI BATISTA SALVI) ; born, 1605 ; died, 1685. *Roman School.*

Born at Urbino; studied first under his father, Tarquinio Salvi, but completed his art education at Rome and Naples, where he is said to have been a pupil of **Dominichino**, but little is known with certainty as to his history, although he painted much, and his pictures are to be found in all the best Continental galleries. In his larger and more original subjects he is distinguished by a dry, cold, and staringly clear style of colouring, every part of the picture being very distinctly made out; but his small heads of the Madonna, of which he painted a great number, have a good deal of depth of tone, and a softness that seems as though imitated from Correggio. The two pictures described below fairly illustrate the two manners alluded to.

83. Head of the Madonna.

Replica of a well-known picture at Florence—the face half in shadow, looking out from below dark blue drapery with a sad expression, though not a Mater Doloroso, the hands clasped.

Formerly in the Koncheleff Besborodeo collection ; purchased for the Gallery in Paris, 1869.

93. *The Madonna and Infant Saviour seated in clouds.*

This group, which is almost line for line a copy from the chief group in Raphael's Madonna da Foligno, or rather from Mark Antonio's engraving from it, as the latter has the two little cherubs on each side, is a fine example of the master's bright dry manner.

Purchased for the Gallery at Milan, 1873.

SCHAUFFELEIN, (HANS); born at Nordlingen; died 1540. *Early German School.*

He was a pupil of Albert Durer, and in many of his works imitated the manner of his master successfully. He is very unequal; many of his works being but slight productions. Among his pictures preserved in Nuremberg, a St. Brigid, in the Chapel of St. Maurice, is commended by Kugler, as being prettily and neatly painted, and having some pretension to grandeur of style. The subject of "Christ mocked," a work of the year 1517, an animated picture of very large size, painted on the wall in tempera, is in the Castle. "The History of Judith," is also there, as well as in the Town Hall of Nordlingen, painted in tempera. His finest work in his native town, the chief theatre of his performance, is an altar-piece, executed in 1521 for Nicholas Ziegler, Vice-Chancellor of Charles V. Kugler writes of it, "the centre, a pieta, is in point of feeling, sense of beauty, and clearness of golden tone, one of the finest pictures of the German school of that period." The clever designs for the woodcuts in the *Teuerdank*, are by his hand.—See further in "Kunst and Künstler in Deutschland," vol. i. pp. 349 and 355.

16. *The Visitation.*

1 ft. 4 in. H., 1 ft. 1 in. w. On panel.

This picture represents Mary's journey into the hill country to a city of Judea, and her arrival at the house of Zacharias and Elizabeth, his wife, as related in St. Luke, chap. 1. It formed part of an altar-piece evidently; as on the back are two saints, St. Anthony and probably St. John, painted *en grisaille*, as was the habit of the time; dated on front and back, 1520.

Purchased in London, 1863.

SCHIAVONE, (ANDREA) ; born in Sebenico, in Dalmatia, in 1522; died, 1582. *Venetian School.*

His parents, who had established themselves in Venice, were very poor, and unable to place him, as they wished, under the direction of a good master. Andrea, however, copied the engravings of Parmigianino, and the works of **Giorgione** and Titian; but, unfortunately, from his poverty he was obliged to paint for bread before he was well grounded in the knowledge of design, and only under the patronage of some house and wall painters, who were able to recommend him and employ him as an assistant. Titian obtained leave for him to work, along with others, in ornamenting the library of St. Mark, where he drew more correctly, perhaps, than in any other place. Tintoretto, also, often assisted him in his labours, to observe his manner of colouring, and praised it highly. Still, it is said that he lived in misery, and did not leave enough of money to bury him ; but after his death his fame increased, and his paintings were removed from the chests and benches on which they were originally painted, to adorn the cabinets of connoisseurs. His works had much elegance and spirit, and his colours were beautiful. Some biographers have given him the name of Medulo or Medola, but this seems to be very uncertain.

Others, calling him Meldolla, have confounded him with Andrea Meldolla, who engraved a great number of Parmigianino's works. There was also a Gregorio Schiavone, called, by mistake, Girolamo, who painted, from 1460 to 1490, in a style resembling Mantegna and G. Bellini, and a Luca Schiavone, a good painter of decorations, working in Milan in 1450.

A Sketch. Mythological Subject.
Idem.

7¼ in. h., 7¼ in. w.   Both on canvas.

Purchased with the remainder of the Beaucousin collection in 1859, and deposited by the Trustees of the National Gallery, London.

SCHWARTZ, (CHRISTOPHER); born, 1550; died, 1597.

He taught at Munich, and Lüster was one of his pupils. Christopher Schwartz was one of those masters of the German School who applied themselves particularly to the study of Italian art, and especially to the colouring of the Venetians; and he is said to have formed his style on that of Titian, in Venice. He is often confounded with M. Schoevaerdts, who lived in the middle of the seventeenth century. [See No. 104, BRUYN.]

SEBASTIANO DEL PIOMBO; born at Venice, 1485, died at Rome 1547. *Venetian School.*

His proper name was Luciani, but he was commonly called Sebastiano del Piombo from his office as Keeper of the Leaden Seals under Clement VII. His first profession was music, but he devoted himself to painting. and acquired the first principles of that art from Giovanni Bellini, whom, however, he soon deserted to place himself under Giorgione, the vividness and harmony of whose colouring delighted him, and with whom he remained long enough to imbibe much of his feeling for colour. He was invited to Rome by Agostino Ghigi, about 1512; was much esteemed by Michel Angelo, who employed him to paint many of his designs, and in return is said to have aided him by designs in many of his paintings. Admittedly his greatest work is the "Raising of Lazarus," now in the National Gallery of London, which he painted in rivalry with Raphael in his last and greatest work, the "Transfiguration." Michel Angelo is said to have aided him in the design of this work; and the figure of Lazarus is evidently Michel Angelo's design. Vasari writes that from the period he assumed the office of Frate del Piombo he neglected his art and gave himself up to "good cheer" and to society, for which he was peculiarly fitted by his powers of conversation and his musical talents.

80. Saint Bartholomew.

5 ft. 7 in. h., 3 ft. 3 in. w.

Small life-size, whole length. The Saint looks up, his left hand crosses his body, and the hand rests upon an open book upon his right knee; in the right hand he holds the knife, his attribute as being the instrument of his martyrdom.

78. Saint John the Evangelist.

5 ft. 7 in. h., 3 ft. 3 in. w.

The Saint, with his left hand upon his breast, and head inclined to the right shoulder, looks out of the picture; in his right hand he bears the martyr-palm, commemorative of his having been immersed in boiling oil, from which he was miraculously preserved.

These two pictures have been attributed to Sebastian de Piombo, though Waagen attributes them to Moretto di Brescia.

Purchased at the sale of Archdeacon Thorpe's collection, at Durham, in 1863.

SESTO, CESARE DA ; (or CESARE MILANESE), flourished from 1500 to 1524. *Florentine School.*

He was esteemed one of the best pupils of Leonardo da Vinci, and was intimate with Baldassare Peruzzi, and Raphael, whom he is said to have rivalled, for some time, in easel pictures. Raphael is reported once to have said to him, " It is strange that, being bound in such strict ties of friendship as we two are, we do not in the least respect each other with our pencils;" as if they had been on a sort of equality. Lomazzo holds up Cesare da Sesto as a model in design, in attitude, and particularly in the art of using his lights. Lanzi mentions having seen a copy of an Herodias described by Lomazzo as the work of Cesare da Sesto, and says that the countenance bore a strong resemblance to Raphael's Fornarina. The original, at the first occupation by the French, was adjudged to Madame la Pagine, wife of General Buonaparte, and passed into France. Many other important works of his pencil exist in Italy, but they are very rare in European collections. Some of his works are so beautiful in softness, brightness, and harmony of colouring, that they might have easily been ascribed to Raphael himself. He painted in the landscapes of his friend, Bernazzano, fables and histories, in which he displayed all his power.

115. *The Madonna, with the Infant Christ and Saint John.*

3 ft 2 in. H., 2ft. 5 in. w. On panel.

Christ holds a small bird upon his hand—emblem of spiritual life—which St. John holds out his hand to take. A green curtain is disposed behind the Virgin's head, and a small glass vase with flowers stands near.

Purchased in Rome, October, 1856, for the National Gallery of Ireland.

SMITH (CATTERSON, R.H.A.) ; born, 1806 ; died, 1872. *British School.*

Born at Shipton in Yorkshire. He came to Ireland in 1839, residing at Londonderry, and settling in Dublin in 1844, where he enjoyed until his death, the first position as a portrait painter. Was soon afterwards elected a member of the Royal Hibernian Academy, of which he became President in 1859, and with one year's interval retained that distinction until he resigned it in 1866.

141. *Portrait of William Dargan* ; born, 1799 ; died, 1867.

To whose munificence was due the great Dublin Exhibition of 1853, which was carried out at his sole cost, and to commemorate which, and as a testimonial to him, the fund was raised and the project started, out of which the National Gallery of Ireland has grown. This picture was painted for it by the order of the Board of Governors and Guardians.

In Historical and Portrait Gallery.

122. *Portrait of Himself.*

An unfinished picture, but painted with great force and firmness, and an admirable likeness.

Purchased for the Gallery in Dublin, 1873.

In Historical and Portrait Gallery.

SNYDERS, SNEYDERS, or SNYERS, (FRANS); born at Antwerp in 1579; died in 1657. *Flemish School.*

He studied under Peter Breughel in 1593, and subsequently under Van Balen. At first he painted fruit and flowers, and afterwards devoted himself to the study of animals of every kind, which he painted with a truth of drawing, vigour of colour, and lightness of pencil which few artists have equalled and none have surpassed. Philip III. of Spain commissioned him to paint scenes of the chase and battlepieces ; and the Archduke Albert, Governor of the Low Countries, named him his principal painter, and loaded him with honours and gifts. Snyders frequently painted animals, flowers, and fruit in the pictures of Rubens and Jordaens, who in turn painted figures in his works. He also painted larders, kitchens, dead game; but his great fame is derived from his boar and stag hunts, and his wonderful power in delineating animals. A very fine portrait of Snyders by Van Dyck was formerly in the Orleans collection, and is now in that of the Earl of Carlisle, at Castle Howard.

25. *Boar Hunt.*

4 f. 2 in. H., 6 f. 8½ in. w. On canvas.

The boar is in his lair ; one dog turns upon a bank snarling at him, while another makes off, evidently having received his death-wound. This work, though somewhat slight and sketchy, bears the stamp of originality.

Purchased in London in 1864.

STEENWYCK, STEINWYCK, or STEINWEYCK, the Younger (HENDRIK VAN); born at Amsterdam in 1589, died in London, date unknown ; but pictures of his are known, dated 1642. *Dutch School.*

He was a pupil of his father, Hendrik Van Steenwyck the elder, whom he surpassed by superior delicacy of execution and clearness of colour. He painted architectural scenes, but principally interiors of churches, where he showed great knowledge of perspective. He was fond of night effects, and frequently represented interiors lighted with flambeaux. J. Breughel, M. Van Thulden, Stalbem, Poelenburg, and Van Bassen have often painted figures in his pictures. He worked a good deal in England. Van Dyck, who had a high opinion of his talent, and who employed him to paint architecture in the backgrounds of his portraits, presented him to Charles I., for whom he executed many paintings. After his death, his widow established herself in Amsterdam, and painted perspective views in the same style.

7. *Palace of Dido.*

1 ft. 3 in. H., 2 ft. 3 in. w. On copper.

A group of figures occupies the foreground of an extensive terrace, while long colonnades stretch away from the spectator, and distant pleasure-grounds are seen beyond.

Bequeathed to the nation by Lieut.-Colonel Ollney. Deposited by the Trustees of the National Gallery, London.

STOTHARD, (THOMAS, R.A.) ; born, 1755 ; died, 1834. *British School.*

Born in London. He was originally employed in designing patterns for brocaded silks, but at an early age began to illustrate books for London publishers, and gradually attracted notice, and became first a student and afterwards an exhibitor at the Royal Academy, of which he was elected an associate in 1785, and academician in 1794, and librarian in 1812. He is distinguished beyond all other artists of the British School, by inexhaustible fertility of invention, great refinement of conception, and grace of pencil. He is said to have made 5,000 designs, 3,000 of which have been engraved, and it would not be easy to find one of them from which these rare qualities are absent. He was an excellent colourist, taking Rubens, for whom he had an unbounded admiration, for his model, and a correct draughtsman. It need not be added that he showed an example of steady and untiring industry. His reputation never stood higher than of late years.

154. *The Judgment of Paris* (attributed to).

[See RUBENS, page 94.]

4 ft. 9 in. H., 6 ft. 1 in. w.

A copy from the celebrated picture in the National Gallery, formerly in the Orleans collection. Those who are conversant with the touch and manner of Stothard will easily recognise it in this fine reproduction of his favourite master.

Presented to the Gallery by WILLIAM LECKY BROWN, esq. (In Modern Gallery).

SUSTERMANS, or SUTTERMANS (JUSTUS) ; born at Antwerp, in 1597 ; died, 23 April, 1681.

He was the scholar of Willem de Vos in Antwerp, and worked with Frans Pourbus the younger, in Paris. In 1620 he established himself in Florence, and entered the service of the Grand Duke Cosmo II., and of his successors, Ferdinand II. and Cosmo III. He received a yearly salary of 25 scudi, besides apartments and maintenance in the palace, and payment for all his works. In 1624 Sustermans was invited to Vienna to paint the portraits of the Imperial family ; and in 1627 he visited Rome, and painted the portrait of Pope Urban VIII., who presented him with the Cross of Malta. His reputation was now European : in 1638 he received the great picture of "Tragedy," or "The Horrors of War," sent to him by Rubens from Antwerp ; in 1641 he exchanged portraits with Vandyck ; in 1645 he was summoned to Rome to paint Innocent X. ; and in 1649 he accompanied the Cardinal Giovanni Carlo de' Medici to Spain, in the suite of the Queen of Philip IV. Among the numerous distinguished sitters of Sustermans were Galileo, and Viviani the mathematician. He was three times married, and left a considerable fortune at his death, comprising an extensive collection of pictures and other works of art, including the large picture by Rubens above-mentioned, now in the Pitti Palace.

54. *Portraits—Supposed to represent Ferdinando II., Duke of Tuscany, and his wife, Vittoria della Rovere.*

4 ft. 8 in. H., 4 ft. 2 in. w. On canvas.

This picture was formerly attributed to Velazquez. Three-quarter length, life size.

Engraved by W.Holl, for Jones's National Gallery.

Formerly in the Angerstein collection, with which it was purchased for the nation in 1824.

Deposited by the Trustees of the National Gallery, London.

TENIERS, DAVID, the YOUNG ; born at Antwerp in 1610; died at Perk village, between Malines and Alonde, in 1694. *Flemish School.*

He was pupil of his father, David the Elder ; some say afterwards of Adrian Brouwer, and of Rubens, but these points are contested. He was certainly intimate with Rubens, and his first wife was Anne Breughel daugh-

ter of Velvet Breughel, to whom Rubens stood in the relation of master
and guardian. At first he was not successful, and the works of inferior
artists, Van Thilborg Artois and Van Heil, were preferred to his. Fortune,
however, soon favoured him, and few artists enjoyed greater or more
deserved popularity. Archduke Leopold was his first patron; he named
him court painter, chamberlain, and director of his picture gallery, and
sent many of his works to the several courts of Europe, whereby his
reputation was extended. The King of Spain admired his works so much
as to construct a gallery solely for their reception. Queen Christiana of
Sweden obtained some of his works, and recompensed him liberally,
sending him, besides, her own portrait with a chain of gold. Don Juan
of Austria was the pupil and friend of Teniers. Such was the demand
for his works that although he painted with marvellous rapidity, often
commencing and finishing a picture in the same day, he could not meet
the demands of the nobles and art lovers of the country. He acquired
a considerable fortune, and built a chateau in the village of Perk, where
it is said he studied the habits of peasant life, and brought about him in
social intercourse the nobles and most distinguished men in literature, the
sciences, and arts. Although Teniers painted large works, he excelled in
compositions of moderate cabinet size. His kermesses, or village fêtes, his
landscapes, smoking booths, card-players, guard-rooms, chemists, and
quacks, silvery in tint and touched with a light and vivid pencil, exhibit
great power and originality. He executed imitations of other masters,
termed *pasticci*, with great effect : but it is believed that many of these supposed imitations were but able copies of works in the Archduke Leopold's
collection. The fine examples of his power bring very large prices.

23. *Hustle Cap.*

9 in. H., 1 f. 1 in. w.   On panel.

A man seated at a table shuffles a hat in which coins are placed
while others interested in the game look on. The principal
figure sits without his coat, in his shirt sleeves; other figures are
represented round the fire-place in the background smoking.

Formerly in the Harberton collection, and purchased at the sale of that
collection, in London, in 1864.

Peasants Merrymaking.

[In the large landscape by Lucas Van Uden.]

The figures put in with the greatest spirit and masterly freedom.
The chief couple, who are dancing a kind of jig, have extraordinary
life ; while the old fellow on the left inviting the milkmaid to
dance, and her figure and brass milk-can, show great brilliancy of
touch. The old grey-bearded piper, who, from the frequent
portraits of him to be found in Tenier's pictures of his own
family and chateau, was probably a retainer, is standing making
music for the dancers, of whom an eager couple are running down
the hill towards him. The delicate harmony of colour in all
these figures is very pleasing to the eye, and admirably adapted
to relieve the large masses of green and brown which pervade the
picture. Near the foot of the woman dancing may be found the
monogram of the artist.

TIEPOLO, (GIOVANNI BATISTA) ; born, 1693 ; died, 1770. *Venetian
School.*

A Venetian painter of the later period, who imitated, at a very great distance, the manner and general style of Veronese, but was much more artificial in composition, and paler in his colouring, which has a meretricious character. He was chiefly employed in the decoration of churches and palaces in fresco, and was in great fashion in his day, being invited to the Court of Madrid, where he was employed by the king. He died there in 1770.

74. Elijah invoking, by Prayer, the Sacred Fire from Heaven.

2 ft. 6½ in. H., 4 ft. 8 in. w.   On canvas.

This is an oval composition sketch for a ceiling picture. A great pyramid of stairs rises up in the centre of the picture, on which stands King Achab, with upraised head and hands—Elijah at his altar, praying, "Hear me, O Lord, hear me, that this people may learn that thou art the Lord God," while the fire of the Lord descends from heaven on the pure sacrifice, to the confusion of the false priests and worshippers of Baal.—III. Book of Kings, chapter xviii.

Purchased in Dublin, 1859.

TINTORETTO. [See ROBUSTI.]

UDEN, (LUCAS VAN); born, 1595 ; died, 1662. *Flemish School.*

Born at Antwerp; the son of a painter of little repute, who gave him his first teaching ; he distinguished himself early by his love of nature, and his indefatigable study of all her various phases of wood, sky, and cloud, and gained great repute in his native city, where his works attracted the admiration of Rubens, who frequently employed him to paint the background of his pictures, and in return often put in the figures for him in his landscapes, as did also Teniers, Jordaens, and others. His early style seems to be founded upon Velvet Breughel, but he seems to have developed more breadth and strength of handling under the influence of Rubens, to whom some of his pictures are often attributed.

41. An extensive Woody Landscape, with Peasants Merrymaking.

3 ft. 6 in. H., 6 ft. 10 in. w.

The combined work of Van Uden and Teniers ; this picture gives a very good idea of the characteristic qualities of the former, great part of it being in the style of Rubens, while parts, more especially in the extreme distance, remind one forcibly of Breughel. The scene is probably in the neighbourhood of Antwerp, the house in the distance resembling the chateau of Teniers, as often introduced into his own pictures. The scene of country life is very English in its character, as one may imagine it in the olden time ; the squire's house snugly buried in trees, the parish church at a short distance from it, and the home farm almost equally near, with the cultivated land, and hedge-divided fields. Signed with the full autograph in the left corner.

Purchased for the Gallery, in London, 1874.

VANNUCCHI, (ANDREA); called ANDREA DEL SARTO ; born at Florence, 1488 ; died there, 1530. *Florentine School.*

Andrea, called Del Sarto (the son of the tailor), from his father's profession, was placed at seventeen years of age as apprentice to a goldsmith

whom he soon left to study drawing with Gio. Barile, a skilful carver in wood
but an inferior painter.   He afterwards entered the studio of Pietro di
Cosimo, and studied with ardour the works of Massaccio and Ghirlandajo, of Leonardo da Vinci, and Michel Angelo.   Andrea and his friend
and intimate, **Franciabigio**, had for some time a studio in common between
them, and executed together many works.   In a few years he made great
progress, and painted a considerable number of pieces, almost all on religious subjects, his style being so full of sweetness and elegance that in his
own time he was surnamed " Andrea the Faultless;" and he would have
become very prosperous but for the violence and caprice of his wife,
Lucrezia del Fede, who was a source of continual misfortune to him.
Vasari says, that from the time of his marriage with her he was abandoned
by his employers and despised by his friends, and that she drove away all
his scholars.   In 1518 Andrea went to France, invited by Francis I.,
where honours were heaped upon him, and he was magnificently rewarded
for his works.   He might have enjoyed a brilliant fortune at the French
court, but for the complaining letters of his wife, which induced him to
return to her.   He left France, solemnly pledging himself to return, and
intrusted by the king with a sum of money to be expended for him in
the acquisition of objects of art.   This money he disgracefully wasted in
his own or his wife's extravagance ; and though he afterwards repented
deeply, and exerted all his energy, he could never regain his former reputation ; and so he lived miserably till 1530, when he died of the plague
abandoned by his wife and by every attendant, in the 42nd year of his age.

98. *The Adoration of the Magi.*

3 in. H., 1 ft. 9½ in. w.   On panel.

This little picture was either a panel in some altar decoration, or
else formed part of a domestic cabinet, such as it was the custom
at the time to have ornamented by even the greatest painters.

Purchased in Rome, October, 1856, for the National Gallery of Ireland.

103. *A Pieta and two Saints in a Predella.*

Pieta—8½ in. H., 1 ft. 6½ in. w.   Saints—7 in. H., 7 in. w.   On panel.

This Predella contains in the centre a Pieta, with St. John supporting the head of the dead Christ, and Mary Magdalene weeping
at His feet.   In the right compartment St. Peter, in the left St.
Appolonia.   Originally six other Saints were contained in the
Predella, which belonged to the family of Menichini, at Perugia.

Purchased in Rome in 1864.

104. *Case containing four of the six Saints referred*
to under the foregoing number, as originally
belonging to the same Altar-piece in Perugia.

The Saints represented here are St. Francis, St. Lawrence, St.
Jerome, and St. Dominick.

These exquisite little pictures are distinguished by a charm of
freshness of handling and sentiment of colour scarcely equalled
in the larger and more finished works of the master.

Two others are in the possession of the Earl of Warwick.

Purchased in Rome in 1865.

VAROTARI, (ALESSANDRO) ; called IL PADOVANINO, poet, painter, and engraver ; born at Padua, 1590; died, 1650. *Venetian School.*

His father, Doria Varotari, a good painter, born at Verona, gave him some instructions; but he died when Alessandro was a child. The boy shortly after set out for Venice, and soon began to distinguish himself there, taking Titian as his particular model, and penetrating, gradually, so far into this great master's peculiar character, that he is preferred by many to any other of Titian's disciples. He was remarkable for the grace and beauty of his women and boys, and the dignity of his heroic pieces ; he also succeeded admirably in landscapes. His sister, Chiara Doria, was a good portrait painter, and his son, Dario, was a painter, poet, and engraver, and besides, a physician.

87. *Œneus and Meleager.*

6 ft. 5 in. H., 7 ft. 9 in. w. On canvas.

According to the mythological Grecian history, it happened to Œneus (King of Calydon in Ætolia), that in a general harvest sacrifice to all the Gods, he forgot Diana, the Goddess of the Chase ; upon which Diana, indignant at his neglect, denounced vengeance against him, and sent into Calydon a huge boar to devastate the country. For several years the people of Calydon, assisted by the neighbouring tribes, endeavoured to destroy the monster, but without success ; till at last Meleager, the young son of King Œneus, grew up, and a great hunt was organized, in which, under his leadership, all the adventurous youths of the country took part, and the boar was finally killed by Meleager's spear. The subject of the picture seems to be the appearance of the Goddess Diana, in person, before Œneus, at a feast ; threatening her vengeance for his neglect of her divinity.

Purchased in Rome, 1856, for the National Gallery of Ireland.

The Madonna and Infant Christ. (After Titian).

2 ft. 9 in. H., 2 ft. 2 in. w.

This seems a copy of a group, or part of the picture by Titian, No. 635 in National Gallery in London. A similar work is in Hampton Court, No. 409, and has upon it a similar coat of arms, bearing *argent, a tower gules, thereon two batons fleurs de lis in saltier,* which Mrs. Jameson says are those of the Torriani family.

Purchased in Dublin in 1860 for the National Gallery of Ireland.

VECCHIA, (PIETRO DELLA). [See MUTTONI, No. 55.]

VECELLIO, (TIZIANO) ; born in the town of Pieve, chief town of the ancient province of Cadore, in 1477 ; died of the plague, the 27th August, 1576. (*Venetian School.*)

He showed from the earliest period the greatest propensity for painting, and learned, it is said, the first elements of drawing from Antonio Rossi, a painter of his country. About ten years of age his father sent him to Venice, in order to continue his studies. Titian studied first under Gentili Bellini, then under Giovanni, his brother, with whom he appears to have remained until he was eighteen or twenty years of age. He commenced by imitating his master, and painted in his somewhat formal manner, a great number of subject pictures and of portraits. Soon, however, he enlarged his style, and emulated his co-disciple, Giorgione, contending the palm with him in works on the façade of the Fondaco de' Tedeschi at Venice in 1507. After the death of Giorgione, Titian, then without a rival, was commissioned to complete the painting in the ducal palace, left unfinished by that great artist. After the death of Giov. Bellini, he was put in possession of an annual pension of 100 ducats, which he had possessed from la Senseria del Fondaco de' Tedeschi, for painting in the great Council Hall the Battle of the Venetians at Cadore. He painted for the Church de' Frari, at Venice, his celebrated Assumption, which was placed over the chief altar the 20th May, 1518, and a great number of other works about the same time, which perished in the fire of the ducal palace in 1577. Charles V. having come to Rome, in order to be crowned as Emperor by Clement VII., Titian, by the recommendation of his great friend, Aretin, was summoned to court to paint his portrait. Thenceforth Titian's works were amply rewarded, above all by the Emperor, who took him into high favour, and his career was one long triumph. His industry and zeal abated not with his advance in years; and when Henry III. quitted the throne of Poland, and passing through Venice, previous to taking possession of the throne of France, visited Titian in 1574 at his own house, he found him occupied at a picture which he wished to have placed over his tomb—a picture subsequently finished by Palma (Il Giovanne), and now in the Academy of Venice. Titian ranks as the first of colourists, and his drawing shows knowledge combined with refinement and nature. He was great in landscape, and no one has surpassed him in portraiture. He was cherished by princes and potentates, and numbered among his friends the illustrious personages of his age. He painted until his last hour ; and even when dying of the plague at ninety-nine years of age, he is said to have exclaimed, that "he only began to comprehend what painting was." His scholars and followers were numerous. He had a brother, a son, and a nephew, painters of some note. Nearly all the Venetian artists frequented his school. Of the Flemish artists, Jean Calcar, Barent, and Lambert Zeustris, imitated his manner perfectly, and multiplied his pictures by fine copies, which he frequently retouched.

84. *The Supper of Emmaus.*

A design similar in general arrangement to the famous picture in the Louvre—and to that in Lord Yarborough's collection, which differs slightly from both—but varied in all details, the heads, especially, having a distinct character of their own, and being apparently portraits. It is thus described in the catalogue of the Demidoff collection, sold in Paris in 1870. This important picture by Titian, after having belonged to several of the Patrician Galleries of Venice, became, towards 1836, the property of the Abbate Celotti, a connoisseur and writer upon art, who remarks that Titian has in this version shown himself more faithful to the text of the Evangelist than in other representations of the same subject. "But they restrained Him saying, stay with us because it is towards evening." The picture became the property of the late Prince Demidoff in 1836, and continued until 1870 to form one of the chief attractions of his collection at the Villa San Donato near Florence. It was sold with the rest of his collection in that year at Paris, and was then purchased for the National Gallery of Ireland. Although some parts of this picture quite come up to one's expectation from the greatest of colourists, yet it is not equally satisfactory throughout, notably the principal head is inferior, apparently having suffered from restoration ; nothing can be finer than the evening glow in the sky behind the old disciple, just throwing a last gleam upon the tower on the opposite side, or than the handling of the tablecloth and the still life that is on it. In the background the outline of the Dolomite mountains may be recognised, which were within view of Titian's birthplace, and which he so often introduced into his pictures. There is a beautiful engraving of this picture by Roselli in the Gazette des Beaux Arts.

The frame of this picture is a remarkable specimen of modern Florentine design and carving, bringing in objects appropriate to the subject. The style is very florid and not in the best taste.

VELAZQUEZ, (Don Diego Rodriguez de Silva); born at Sevilla, in Spain, 6th June, 1599; died at Madrid, 7th August, 1660. *Spanish School.*

He was first taught by Herrera the elder, and afterwards by Fran. Pacheco. He studied closely the Italian and Flemish paintings, which, about this period, began to appear in Seville, and in an especial manner the works of Luis Tristan de Toleda, whose style, warmed by that of the Flemish masters, had nothing of the coldness and dryness of Velazquez' former teachers. In 1622 he went to Madrid, and the next year Philip IV. attached him to his court. This king was so much charmed by his talent, that he soon created him his own painter, with other appointments in the palace, and about his person; and he fixed a sum of 1,000 ducats as his pension, independently of the price of his works. Rubens, on his visit to Madrid in 1628, advised Velazquez not to confine himself to mere portrait painting, but to attempt great subjects, and to travel in Italy. Velazquez took this advice, and went to Venice in 1629, where he studied the colourists, and then to Rome, where he copied a great part of the Last Judgment of M. Angelo, and the School of Athens and Parnassus of Raphael. He afterwards visited Naples, and returned to Madrid in 1631. After this time he was looked on as the first painter in Spain. He remained at the Court of Madrid for seventeen years (except during two excursions into the province of Aragon). In 1648 he was sent by Philip IV. to purchase, in Italy, objects of art for an academy which that king wished to found. It was during this journey that he painted the so much admired portrait of the Pope, Innocent X. He visited several of the Italian cities, and wished much to go to Paris; but the breaking out of war between France and Spain prevented his executing this project. He accordingly returned to Madrid, where he remained till 1660. In March, in this year, he accompanied Philip IV. and his daughter, Maria Teresa, the betrothed of Louis XIV., to Irun, where he designed, in the "Isle of Pheasants," the pavilion in which the two kings met; but he died on his return to Madrid, from this journey, at the age of 64. Velazquez painted fruits, flowers, animals, interiors, landscapes, portraits, and historical scenes, and excelled in all these styles. His portraits alone would suffice to render his name illustrious. He is perhaps the only Spanish artist who has very seldom represented religious subjects.

14. *Portrait of the Infanta Donna Maria of Austria, Daughter of Philip IV.*

2 ft. 10 in. H., 1 ft. 11 in. w. On canvas.

The Infanta is represented at full length looking to the spectator; her right hand resting on the back of a chair, in her left a handkerchief. The face, at no time very pleasing, has suffered by cleaning. This is the Infanta who was the object of King Charles's visit to Madrid.

Purchased in Madrid in 1864.

34. *A Legend of Saint Benedict.*

(Attributed to.)

A very dark, highly finished picture in Velazquez' early manner, if by him. The saint is represented apparently taking small dead fishes from a dish held by a young man at his side, and placing them in a fountain of water, which brings them to life again ; a youth on his left looks on in an attitude of astonishment. Purchased for the Gallery, at Leeds, in 1868.

VELDE, (WILLIAM VAN DEN THE ELDER); born, 1610 ; died, 1693, *Dutch School.*

A native of Leyden ; he was in early life a sailor, but before he reached the age of twenty began to be known for his clever marine sketches in black and white, and soon afterwards was employed by the Government of the States of Holland, who, to assist and encourage him in his study of naval subjects, allowed him the use of a government yacht to enable him to accompany the fleets and follow their movements, which he did even during battles, having thus been present in several historical actions. After the Restoration he was invited to England by King Charles II., and regularly employed by his Majesty, by King James II., and by William III., until his death. He was the father and master of the more famous William Van de Velde the younger, who accompanied him to England, and was employed to assist him in the colouring of his " draughts," to use the quaint expression of the Royal Order, at an equal salary, viz., £100 a year, as that assigned to his father.

58. *The Embarkation of King Charles II., on his return to England after the Restoration.*

3 ft. 7 in. h., 5 ft. 10 in. w.

The scene is represented with great life and spirit by the painter, who doubtless .was present. The large man-of-war, with the Royal Standard flying at the masthead, which is to receive His Majesty, is in the middle distance, the sails being unfurled, and other ships making ready to start, while the sea is covered with boats, either conveying passengers on board the fleet or with spectators to witness its start ; the king is just about to ascend the companion ladder, and the sailors in the rigging above are seen cheering and waving their caps. The sea is rough and the whole scene is expressive of great life and movement ; portions of the picture, especially in the extreme distance, are painted with so much delicacy as to suggest the belief that the hand of the younger Van de Velde is traceable, and that it may be one of those pictures that are alluded to in the royal order mentioned above.

Purchased for the Gallery, in London, 1874.

VERONESE, (PAOLO CALIARI). [See CALIARI, Nos. 113 & 185.

VIOLA, (GIOVANNI BATTISTA); born at Bologna, 1576 ; died at Rome, 1622. *Bolognese School.*

He was a scholar of Annibale Carracci, and very successfully adopted his manner of painting landscape. He visited Rome in company with his fellow student, Francesco Albano, and was employed in ornamenting, in conjunction with him, the palaces of the nobility. Many of his landscapes were embellished with figures by Albano. Bryan states that the first of his works which brought him into repute was a large landscape, painted for the Vigna of Cardinal Alessandro Montalto, where Paul Bril was employed at the same time. The grandeur both of the style and subject of Viola's landscape excelled the work of the Fleming, and gained him great reputation. Some of his most admired performances are in the saloon of Apollo, in the Villa Aldobrandini.

Landscape—Jacob wrestling with the Angel.

5 ft. 7 in. H., 7 ft. 1 in. w.   On canvas.

A large tree rises in the centre of the picture, with massive foliage against the sky ; beyond, a river flows through the middle distance. In the middle of a road, which winds up a hill to the right of the picture, Jacob wrestles with the Angel.

Purchased in Rome, in 1856.

WERF (ADRIAN VANDER); born, 1659; died, 1722. *Dutch School.*

Born at Kralinger-Ambacht, near Rotterdam. He acquired his art education chiefly from Eglon Vander Neer, whose smooth high finish he imitated. He is chiefly known from his small very minutely finished pictures of classical subjects. Following Italian traditions in his forms and draperies more than any other painter of the Dutch School, they were greatly admired in his own time, and procured him great emolument and fashion. His portraits are few, and chiefly of persons of great rank or distinction.

26. Portrait of an Old Lady.

A very good specimen of the master's peculiar style. Singular delicacy of finish in the face. The identity of the person represented is not known, but the lady bears a strong resemblance to the portraits of the Electress Sophia.

Presented to the Gallery by VISCOUNT POWERSCOURT, K.P., in 1873.

WESTPHALIAN SCHOOL, (EARLY).   UNKNOWN MASTER.

The Blessed Virgin and Child, (with the Donor.)

3 ft. 10½ in. H., 1 ft. 8 in. w.   On panel ; in oil.

The Blessed Virgin stands in a sort of niche, with the Child in her arms. He leans to the right to bless a young Monk who kneels beside ; a scroll comes from the Monk's lips, beginning, "*Miserere mei, clementissime.*" Two angels hold a crown of red and white roses over the Virgin's head. In early religious pictures, it is very common to find the figures of the persons for whom they were painted introduced, in very small size, kneeling at one side.

Deposited in the Gallery by the Trustees of the National Gallery of London.   [Formerly in the Krüger Collection, at Minden.]

WHEATLY (Francis, r.a.); born, 1740; died, 1801. *British School.*

125. *The Volunteers Meeting in College-green,* 1779.

This historical picture, in the truest sense of the word, having been painted at the time, for the chief actor in the event represented, contains portraits of the following personages :—

The Duke of Leinster, Colonel of the 1st Regiment of Dublin Volunteers.
Sir Edward Newenham, Colonel of the 2nd Regiment.
Right Hon. Luke Gardiner, Colonel of Dublin Light Horse.
Sir John Allen Johnston, Captain of Rathdown Light Horse.
John Fitzgibbon (afterwards Earl of Clare).
The Right Hon. David La Touche.
John Armit, Accountant-General.
Captain Schomberg, r.n.
Councillor Pethard, Captain of Lawyer's Corps.
Councillor Caldbeck, Captain of Goldsmiths' Co.
James Napper Tandy.
Jasper Joly.　　&c.,　　&c.,　　&c.
And the famous Princess Daschkow, who was then travelling in Ireland.

Deposited in the National Gallery of Ireland by His Grace the Duke of Leinster. In Historical and Portrait Gallery.

WILLEMS [living]. *Flemish School.* (See No. 137, GENISSON.)

WILSON (Richard, r.a.); born, 1714; died, 1782. *British School.*

A native of Wales. He rose to a high position in the British School as a landscape painter; his style is characterised by much poetic imagination.

157. *A Landscape Composition.*

Purchased for the Gallery in Dublin, 1872.

ZAMPIERI (Domenico), called Il Domenichino ; born October 21, 1581 ; died, at Naples, April 13, 1611. *Bolognese School.*

After several years of severe study at the school of D. Calvaert, at Bologna, where he was acquainted with Guido, Domenichino went to Parma, to study the Lombard works, and thence to Rome, to enrol himself as a pupil of the Carracci. Domenichino was timid and melancholy by nature, and always diffident of his own powers. He shunned all society, the better to devote himself to his art, and only frequented the public places to observe the expression of every feeling in the countenances of the people, and to commit it to his tablets. Hence he has become one of the most successful of all the masters, in giving the most varied and vivid expression to his pictures. His representations of the Scourging of Christ, in San Gregorio, in Rome, and still more his later works, the Communion of Saint Jerome, and the Martyrdom of Saint Agnes, show his extraordinary genius for depicting the very thoughts and feelings of his figures ; and the accessories of these paintings are exquisitely beautiful and graceful. His frescoes, also, were soft and harmonious, and are the ornaments of many churches in Rome. Albano and Annibale Carracci were his warmest friends and admirers ; but unfortunately he had few others during his lifetime ; and he even suffered the most bitter persecution at the hands of Lanfranco and other rivals. He was invited to Naples, to paint the Church of San Gennaro, and was promised magnificent remuneration for it, as well as protection from the cabal of the Neapolitan painters, who, headed by Spagnoletto and Bellisario, had by violence driven away Annibale Carracci, Guido, and Gessi. They harassed him by calumnies, by secretly mixing injurious ingredients with his colours, and by every malicious fraud; so that Domenichino at last secretly fled from Naples; but he was subsequently persuaded to return, and he again made great progress in the work. Before he could complete it, however, he died, and many believe that he was poisoned. Among his imitators, the most distinguished is **Lionel Spada**, whose works have often been attributed to Domenichino.

Copy of the celebrated St. Cecilia of Raphael in the Gallery of Bologna.

A fine reproduction in the colouring, of which the hand of the copier is more distinctly traceable than that of the original master. (See No.   ).

Presented to the Gallery by VISCOUNT POWERSCOURT, K.P.

UNKNOWN.   Sixteenth century.

17. Portrait of Don Carlos, son of Philip II. of Spain.

3 ft. 6 in. H., 2 ft. 7 in. w.   On canvas.

A youth is here represented in the rich costume of the sixteenth century, and is supposed to be Don Carlos, son of Philip II. of Spain. A short mantle hangs upon his right shoulder; with his right hand he is drawing on the glove on his left, which rests upon his sword handle. From the collection of the Duke Braschi, Rome. A similar picture is engraved in the Galerie de Versailles, attributed to Antonio Moro. This picture attributed to Pulzone is either by Moro or Coello.

Purchased in Rome in 1864.

NATIONAL HISTORICAL, AND PORTRAIT GALLERY.

The pictures, busts, &c., here brought together, are intended to form the nucleus of a collection of portraits and authentic historical pictorial records, comprising not only the portraits of eminent Irishmen and Irishwomen, but also of statesmen and others who were politically or socially connected with Ireland, or whose lives serve in any way to illustrate her history, or throw light on her social or literary or artistic records. It will be added to as opportunities occur, and as the resources at the disposal of the Gallery permit ; but it is hoped that the existence of such a collection in a permanent form, may lead to gifts and deposits which will give it a more rapid development, and enlarge the scope of its public interest and utility. The collection of engravings will be found in the Intermediate (new) Gallery.

A list of the contents of this Gallery is here brought together for the convenience of visitors, who are referred to the foregoing alphabetical catalogue of painters for details.

1. *James, first Viscount Lifford.*

Born, 1709; died, 1789.
Lord Chancellor of Ireland, 1767.

Robert Lucius West.
(After Sir Joshua Reynolds.)

2. *Hugh, Earl of Northumberland (afterwards Duke).*

Born, 1712; died, 1786.
Lord Lieutenant of Ireland, 1763.

Thomas Gainsborough, R.A.

3. *The Right Honorable Edmund Burke.*

Born, 1729; died, 1797.
Statesman, Orator, Author, Patriot, and Philosopher.

James Barry, R.A.

4. *George, Earl of Mount Edgcumbe.*

Vice-Treasurer of Ireland.

Sir Joshua Reynolds, P.R.H.A.

5. *The Volunteers of Ireland Meeting in College-green, with portraits of the Duke of Leinster, &c.*

Francis Wheatly, R.A.

6. *King George II., Queen Caroline, Frederick, Prince of Wales, his son, afterwards King George III., and daughters, the Princess of Hesse, &c.*

William Hogarth.

7. *The Right Honorable Henry Grattan.*

Born, 1750; died, 1820.

Orator and Patriot.

Thomas Alfred Jones, P.R.H.A.

(After Ramsey.)

8. *Murrough O'Brien, Marquis of Thomond.*

Sir Thomas Lawrence, P.R.A.

9. *The Right Honorable Sir Maziere Brady, bart.*

Lord Chancellor of Ireland, &c.

Born, 1796; died, 1871.

Thomas Alfred Jones, P.R.H.A.

10. *Sydney, Lady Morgan.*

Born, 1783; died, 1859.

Authoress.

Berthon

11. *James, first Duke of Ormonde, K.G.*

Born, 1610; died, 1688.

Sir Peter Lely.

12. *Catterson Smith, P.R.H.A.*

Born, 1806; died, 1872.

Himself.

13. *Christopher Moore, R.H.A.*

Born,   ; died, 1862.

The Sculptor.   *John Doyle.*

14. *Samuel Lover, R.H.A.*

Born, 1797; died, 1868.

Painter, Novelist, Musician, and Lyrical Poet.

Harwood.

15. *Thomas Dermody.*

Poet.   *C. Allingham.*

16. *Arthur, 1st Duke of Wellington.*

Born, 1769; died, 1852.

John Lucas.

17. Sir Thomas Wyse.

Born, 1801; died, 1862.

Author, Politician, and Diplomatist.

John Partridge.

18. Sir Henry Lawrence, K.C.B.

Statesman and Soldier.   *Dicksee.*

19. Gustavus, Lord Boyne.

W. Hogarth.

20. William Dargan.

Born, 1799; died, 1867.

Catterson Smith, R.H.A.

22. The Most Reverend Archbishop Murray.

(Marble Bust).   *J. Hogan.*

23. Thomas Moore.

(Marble Bust).

Poet.   *C. Moore, R H.A.*

24. The Right Honorable Richard Sheil.

(Marble Bust).

Born, 1791; died, 1851.

Politician, Orator, Diplomatist.

C. Moore, R.H.A

25. Daniel Maclise, R.A.

(Marble Bust).

Born, 1811; died, 1871.

J. Thomas.

26. Thomas Moore.   (In Crayons).

G. Richmond, R.A

27. Clarence Mangan.   (Drawing).

Poet.   *F. W. Burton, R.H.A.*

28. Professor M'Culloch.   (Pencil Drawing).

F. W. Burton.

29. Thomas Davis.   (In Pencil).

Politician and Poet.   *F. W. Burton.*

30. *W. Harvey.*   (Crayons).

(Naturalist).   *F. W. Burton.*

31. *James, first Duke of Ormonde.*

(In Crayons).   *Sir Peter Lely.*

32. *The Right Hon. Henry Grattan.*

(Drawing in Indian Ink).

Presented by His Grace the Duke of Leinster.

T. Scott.

IN INTERMEDIATE (NEW GALLERY).

ENGRAVINGS.

33. *King William III.*

Sir G. Kneller.

See Catalogue in Index, page 31.

INTRODUCTION

CATALOGUE OF SCULPTURE

NATIONAL GALLERY OF IRELAND.

SCULPTURE must naturally have preceded the art of painting. Modelling in soft clay, which was subsequently baked in the sun or by fire, and carving in wood, were practised in the very earliest periods of human existence. The malleability and fusibility of metals suggested their adaptation to sculptural art long before the use of marble. According to Pliny, Dipœnus and Scyllis, who were born in Crete about 580 years before Christ, were the first to use marble, that of Paros, in their statues. Art, by its force and universality as a language, was made available from the earliest period to teach and to record. If the images, which were devised to realize to the human mind the Deity or His many attributes, were ultimately degraded, through ignorance, into idol worship, there is no reason to conclude that either their authors—the artists who wrought them, or the original preachers or ministers of the several faiths in whose teaching they were employed—intended them as other than representative. And we find, in all ages, that this representative aim has led to the highest excellence in art.

EGYPTIAN sculpture, though it never reached the perfection of Grecian, was the earliest of known development, and the most colossal. More than four thousand years ago the people of Egypt, or, perhaps, more strictly speaking, the monarchs—the Pharaohs and Ptolemies—were raising vast structures—pyramids of everlasting intention—and carving their history, their religion, their habits, even to their modes of construction of those vast piles, on enduring stone, in the universal and undying language of art. It is said that the laws of Egypt, and the subservience of art to religious worship, prohibited the development of its power, in the full expression and

beauty of the human figure. However this may be, there is great
dignity and simplicity in their seated figures, such as the colossal
Memnon, or its representative of less magnitude in the vestibule,
No. XI., Amenophis III. There is also evidence of anatomical
knowledge in the joints and muscles indicated, however slightly.
In their sphinxes and lions we observe great power of generaliza-
tion, to adapt them to architectural combinations. Placidity of
countenance, repose, and simplicity of action characterize all the
statues of the best Egyptian era, the Theban, about nine hundred
years before Christ. Their bas-reliefs were generally incised or sunk
within the face of the stone. This was probably a necessity or an
economy of carving on hard blocks, or designedly done to give greater
effect of outline to these works, seen in the subdued light of the
interiors of their temples or tombs, and intended for the embellish-
ment of colour.

Of ASSYRIAN SCULPTURE, Duchêsne (aîné), in his Introductory
Essay to the Statues in the Musée Français, writing some fifty years
back, observes:—" The want of specimens prevents any opinion
being formed on the state of art among the Assyrians ; but it is a
fact known to history, that Babylon was adorned with sculpture ;
and Diodorus Siculus mentions more than three hundred statues at
Nineveh and other cities." Since then Botta and Layard have
explored the grass-grown mounds of Assyria, and have brought to
light the hidden treasures of Babylon and Nineveh, thus confirming
the accuracy of the remote historian, and supplying the links required in the history of sculpture. The Assyrian empire fell two
thousand five hundred years ago, and Nineveh ceased to be a city.
So rapidly did ruin succeed its fall, that two hundred and fifty
years afterward, Xenophon crossed those plains with a vast
army, without referring in his Anabasis to aught but a few ruins.
These great sculptures referred to by historians, and a multitude of
bas-reliefs so recently discovered, are interesting not only in an
archæological and historical point of view, but equally so in point
of art. The few specimens brought together here, exhibit, in the
bas-relief, great skill and sharpness of execution ; and in the
colossal winged-human-headed lions and bulls—embodiments of
mental and physical power—a breadth of treatment not inferior to
Egyptian art. The bas-reliefs differ from the Egyptian in being all
raised above the surface ; that is, having the ground cut away,
although very slightly, and with little roundness in the raised
parts. In some degree the mode of construction of the buildings
which they adorned, may account for this difference of treatment.
The Egyptians built in solid stone, and carved upon its face ; the
Assyrians built their walls of enormous thickness of sun-burnt
brick or clay, mixed with straw, facing them, internally and exter-
nally, where they desired sculpture, with panels of alabaster or
other stone, on which they carved. Even their great lions and other
colossal figures were so executed. When the upper portions of
these buildings, which were of timber, were demolished by fire, and
all overwhelmed in ruin—a result of their mode of structure may

bo remarked to have been the conservation of the sculptures, in the crumbled brick-earth of the walls; and mounds wore rapidly generated over the debris.

PERSEPOLIS, ELLORA, and other eastern cities, where temples wore excavated out of the solid rock, are more interesting in the elucidation of history, and by their architectural remains, than by any evidence of progress in the art of sculpture.

In GREECE the progress of the art of sculpture is traceable not only through its monuments, but by the historical records of the sculptors themselves. In Egyptian or Assyrian art the monuments record their own histories, or the names of the monarchs under whose auspices they were erected. The names of the sculptors have never reached us. But in Grecian art we are led to a more clear appreciation of the dignity and importance of the art itself by the care with which historians have preserved the names and the peculiar fame of the individual artists. Of these the earliest is Dœdalus, whose name is much mixed up with fiction; nevertheless he is the first sculptor of whom there is certain record, and some bronzes of his are referred to by Flaxman, as being in the British Museum. These and others attributed to his pupil Endœus, though rude in workmanship, are not devoid of force and of intention. From his period to that of Phidias, eight hundred years elapsed, during which a slow but steady progress went on. Dipœnus and Scyllis, the first recorded workers in marble, flourished about five hundred and eighty years before Christ. The ago of Pericles is renowned, beyond all others, for the excellence attained in sculpture. Phidias, to whom Pericles confided the supervision of the erection of the Parthenon, stands forth to all time as the greatest sculptor not only of his own but of any age. The glorious remains of that period, from the Parthenon, Theseum, and Erectheum, mutilated as they arc, are worthy of the most careful study. They exhibit grandeur and variety of conception, generalized truth and marvellous detail, even in the minutest folds of drapery, which have never been surpassed. The great emulators of Phidias were Alcamenes, Critias, Nestocles, and Hegias. Twenty years after we read of Agelades, Callor, Polyletus, Phragmon, Gorgias, Lacon, Myron, Scopas, and Perclius. Of the many renowned sculptors subsequent to this period, Praxiteles was perhaps the greatest. Among his known works arc his two statues of Venus; his Satyr, Cupid, Apollo Sauroctonus, or Lizard Killer, now in tho Louvre; and his Bacchus leaning on a fawn. Many reasons have been assigned for the unparalleled excellence of Grecian sculpture. The facilities of study in the stadium, the erection of portrait statues of the victors, whose physical forms, under a system of scientific training, were near approaches to the true types, have all been advanced, and were doubtless great advantages to the sculptor. But hero-worship was their leading inspiration, and physical beauty the object of national devotion. The master-thought was beauty. While their greatest works are found wedded to architecture, as with tho Assyrians and Egyptians, this marked difference is to be observed, that their sculpture is free from conventional type or geometrical form. Their treatment of ornament is, indeed, always abstract or generalized, to harmonize with the outlines of their buildings, but their gods, men, and lower animals are as truly developed, while in harmony with the architectural surrounding, as if they were destined to be seen as isolated works of sculpture. In illustration compare the Theseus of the Parthenon (No. XLIV.) with the Egyptian statue of Amenophis III. (No. XI.).

The term GRECO-ROMAN, as applied to sculpture, is not intended to refer exclusively to statues executed by Greeks in Rome, nor by Romans themselves under Grecian influence. It includes rather the multitude of statues purely Greek, imported by the Roman conquerors as trophies of war, or the no less numerous repetitions of antique statues executed for them. The same vicissitudes which we have noticed in the early history of painting may be related equally of the sister art. The Romans, intent on conquest, seem never to have devoted their energies to the cultivation of the fine arts. In Southern Italy the Etruscans exhibited a very marked genius for art, and cultivated it sedulously, and with success. Their art has been well handed down by their coins and their vases ; but Pliny mentions, in terms of high praise, works of colossal magnitude, such as an Apollo in bronze, fifty feet high, which was placed in the Palatine Library, belonging to the Temple of Augustus. A bronze statue of a Chimæra, and a life-sized statue of an Orator in a toga, still exist in Florence. The first influence of Grecian art began to be felt among the Romans after the conquest of Macedon, one hundred and sixty-seven years before Christ, when, as Plutarch describes, rich spoils of painting and sculpture were made to subserve the triumphs of Paulus Æmilius. Portraiture became general in the Augustan age. The toga, so frequently selected by sculptors for their draped figures, was appropriate and graceful. But the statues of Roman emperors, in their armour, seem to have been the commencement of an era of difficulty to the sculptor in the carving of mere details, which, managed with whatever skill and power, are far from the true vocation of sculpture.

During the long night of Gothicism, which prevailed from the downfall of the empire in Constantinople to the revival of the arts in the thirteenth and fourteenth centuries, we have few traces of their history. In the fifteenth century, with Ghiberti, Luca della Robbia, Donatello, Pisano, the great artists of the Renaissance, a new art era opened. Sansovino, Bandinelli, Cellini, and others produced works of great merit, but it was with Michel Angelo that Italian sculpture assumed its highest ideality and breadth of form. Raphael has left some few works, which prove that he would have excelled in that art as he did in painting, had longer life been assigned to him. Although Italian art of the Renaissance period stands highest, a no less remarkable development took place throughout Europe. Again decadence set in, until the second revival, of which Canova and Thorswalden were the distinguished leaders.

The specimens of sculpture in the gallery are, with very few exceptions, casts ; but all the new casts have been treated by a process of silicatization which preserves their sharpness and purity, leaving them as nearly as possible facsimiles of the original marbles. For the successful application of silicate and aluminate of potash to the plaster we are indebted to Professor W. K. Sullivan, who, after careful experiment, ascertained the true proportions in which this solution might be applied. The importance of such an application cannot be overrated, as it entirely supersedes the necessity of painting; which, once done, will require to be renewed from time to time, to the detriment of the sharpness and accuracy of the cast.

The arrangement has been designed and carried out as far as possible with the purpose of education. Thus a few of the earliest specimens of Assyrian and Egyptian art are placed in the vestibule, and the eye is led from these gradually to the more refined art of Greece. It has not been sought wholly to dissever these specimens from each other ; on the contrary, it seems rather desirable that the student should have the opportunity of analyzing the principles and practice of these early sculptors, by immediate comparison of their works. Looking at the Assyrian bas-reliefs in the vestibule, in juxtaposition with one or two of the metopes and panels of the frieze from the Parthenon, the most ordinary observer will be struck with the difference of motive and power which they exhibit. The collection is, of course, incomplete, even in the specimens of the antique and mediæval art, and a most important extension is yet to be desired in a choice collection of the works of modern sculptors.

SCULPTURE.

NINEVEH.

I. WARRIORS AT THE CHASE. Mural slab, from the latest excavations at Kouyunjik.

II. WARRIOR ENCOUNTERING A LION. From the same.

III. SCENE IN A SIEGE. Warriors swimming in a river on skins inflated with air, a mode of crossing rivers still practised by the Arabs inhabiting Mesopotamia. From the small Temple of the God of War, Nimroud.

IV. WARRIORS HUNTING THE LION. North-west Palace, Nimroud. This is in every way a remarkable specimen for detail and execution. The wounded lion, in his agony and rage, is finely conceived. It is a peculiarity of the lions represented in these bas-reliefs that there is a claw or hook at the extremity of their tails, which has been referred to by ancient writers, and recently found in a specimen brought to England from countries adjoining Assyria.

V. Two slabs from the North-west Palace of Nimroud, representing the "Sacred Tree," and a king between two eagle-headed and winged figures, which bear in either hand a square vessel and a fir cone. These figures, which occur constantly in the sculptures of Nineveh, are supposed to represent particular deities, such as the god Nisroch, or attributes of God himself; and the tree to be the Tree of Life, "so universally recognised in Eastern systems of Theology." (*Vide* Layard). An inscription in cuneiform character crosses the two slabs. Figures, life size.

VI. Two slabs, representing two winged deitics or priests, who bear in their left hands some mystic flower; the right hands arc raised; a cuneiform inscription at their feet.

VII. Two similar slabs, with the exception that the figures bear the square vessel and fir cone. Inscription at the top. These latter were found adjacent to the human-headed lion. No. X.

VIII. OBELISK. 6 ft. 8 in. H. The original, in black marble, was found in the great mound at Nimroud. It is sculptured with twenty-five bas-reliefs, representing the King of Assyria receiving tribute from conquered nations. Long processions of men and animals, elephants and camels, are seen, and vases of precious metals, rare woods, and other objects, are borne by the men. There are 210 lines of cuneiform inscription, which have been deciphered by Col. Rawlinson and Dr. Hincks. The date of the obelisk is thus fixed at 885 years before Christ.

IX. WINGED HUMAN-HEADED BULL. 9 ft. 5 in. H., 10 ft. W.

X. WINGED HUMAN-HEADED LION. 9 ft. 7 in. H., 9 ft. 5 in. W. These mystic combinations, typical of mental power, physical strength, and ubiquity, were placed at the portals of the various chambers of palaces and temples. While conventional in treatment, they exhibit great skill and knowledge on the part of their sculptors. The originals are in the British Museum.

EGYPTIAN.

XI. BANOFRE, a military chief, at the commencement of the eighteenth dynasty, holding several posts, son of Thoth-hai and Thothsi, entirely enveloped in drapery, seated upon a pedestal with arms crossed ; on it, in cuneiform character, is a dedication to Osiris ; found behind the statue of Memnon at Thebes. The original, in black basalt, in the British Museum. Less than life size.

XII. AMENOPHIS III., by some called Amunothph. Seated colossal figure ; 6 ft. 10 in. H. This is the same king who is represented by the statue known as the Vocal Memnon. His name and titles are inscribed upon the throne he sits upon. It belongs to the best period of Egyptian art. Original, in black granite, in the British Museum.

XIII. HEAD OF PASHT OR BUBASTES, the Egyptian Diana, from the edifice erected by Amenophis III. in the Karnak quarter of Thebes. The original statue, a full length figure seated, is in the British Museum.

GRECIAN.

XIV. STELE OR CIPPUS.

XV. FLEURON, from the Temple of Ceres at Eleusis.

XVB. Bas-relief from ELEUSIS. 7 ft. 7 in. H., 5 ft. 2 in. W. This interesting group in low relief was found about the year 1859, near the Church of St. Zacharias in Eleusis, in the place where, according to Pausanias, the Temple of Triptolemus stood. It represents, according to Overbeck's reading, Ceres, Proserpine, and Triptolemus; the mission of Triptolemus with the gift of the ear of corn, his consecration as the originator of agriculture, and the mysteries of Demeter or Ceres. In the interest of art history, this monument of Attic Art is of the highest importance. It cannot be accounted much later than the Eginetan sculpture, and most likely was contemporaneous with that of the Temple of Theseus at Athens, where the original marble is now.

A brief description of the Parthenon at Athens, from which, in its ruined condition, the great works of sculpture, now in the British Museum, were taken by Lord Elgin, which are here represented by casts, may not be unacceptable. It holds the first rank among the combined architectural and sculptural achievements of mankind. As a monument of these combined arts it is a climax.

The Parthenon, dedicated to Minerva, the virgin goddess of the ancients, and the especial patroness of Athens, was erected during the administration of Pericles, fully 2,000 years ago. Ictinus and Callicrates were the architects, who, under the general guidance of Phidias, were employed in the erection of the temple. Its entire cost is supposed to have been about equal to £700,000 of our money. It is an oblong building of the Doric order, 228 feet long by 101 feet wide, on the level of the colonnade, which extended on all sides of the temple proper, called the cella, within which was the great statue of the goddess Minerva. At the eastern and western end of the building the pediments rise in triangles above the external architrave and frieze surmounting the colonnade. In these pediments were represented, in entire relief, on the eastern the birth of Minerva, on the western the contest of Minerva and Neptune for the soil of Attica. Along the frieze of the colonnade the metopes (see XVI. to XXX.) alternated with the triglyphs. Within the colonnade, along the outer wall of the cella, ran the Panathenaic frieze. (See XXXI. to XLII.)

XVI. to XXX., both numbers inclusive, are casts from the Metopes of the Parthenon, of which the original marbles are in the British Museum. They are set in panels on the wall of the vestibule and sculpture-hall. No. XXIII. on the east wall is placed between two of the triglyphs cast from the Parthenon in order to show the original position. The Metopes represent the battle between the Centaurs and Lapithœ, or rather between the Centaurs and Athenians, who, under Theseus, joined the Lapithæ, a people of Thessaly, in this contest. As a whole, magnificent specimens of art, they are, nevertheless, unequal, some of them being evidently executed by other hands than those of Phidias. They are about 4 feet 2 inches square, and were originally seen at a height of nearly 44 feet from the ground.

XXXI. to XLII., set in panels along the wall of the vestibule and sculpture-hall, under the metopes, are casts from the marbles of the Panathenaic frieze, which ran along the exterior wall of the cella or inner temple of the Parthenon, which are in the British Museum. From their elevated position under the colonnade, they could only receive a reflected light, and be seen at a very acute angle ; the sculptor, therefore, adopted a low relief, in contrast with the metopes, which received the open light of day. It is said that the marbles of the Panathe-

naic frieze were coloured. They extended 380 feet, and represented the whole of the solemn procession to the temple
of Minerva during the great festival, which was held
once in four years, in the third year of each Olympiad.
Every freeborn inhabitant of Attica was entitled to assist at
it. Many are on horseback, others about to mount, some
in chariots, some leading the sacrificial oxen and other vic-
tims ; some bearing offerings, and presenting the sacred veil
in presence of the gods, seated on thrones.

XXXIV. In a frame in the offset from the Sculpture Hall, to the
left of the principal entrance, are three slabs, on which are
represented deities or deified heroes. According to the
editor of " Le Tresor Numismatique," who adopts Brönsted's
reading of these marbles, the four figures to the left are
guardians of the temple, or receivers of the tributes to be
deposited in the Opisthodome, or Treasury ; of the four
figures seated, the two to the left are supposed to represent
Castor and Pollux, and the female figure next to the right,
who bears a long sceptre, is by some called Ceres, by others
Venus. The last figure, seated in an admirably natural
pose, may be Mars or Mercury. Whatever the uncertainty
as to the representative intention of these figures, the group,
from its natural ease and pleasing arrangement, is one of
the most beautiful in the friezes.

XXXVI. Seven of the slabs of the Panathenaic friezes are comprised
in one panel on the eastern wall of the Gallery, in consecutive order; and for action, variety of movement, and consecutive intention, are unequalled in the art of bas-relief. Of
the other compartments no particular notice is required. No
attempt has been made to arrange them according to their
sequence on the frieze, except as far as their action suited.
Wherever two slabs are placed in the same panel, which are
not consecutive, a line of demarcation is given by a narrow
style.

XLIII. Two slabs, not consecutive, from the interior of the cella of
the Temple of Apollo Epicurius (the Deliverer), built on
Mount Cotyliou, near the city of Phigalia, in Arcadia. Pausanias, in his description of this temple, informs us that i t
was erected by Ictinus, architect of the Parthenon, and therefore its sculptures are coeval with those of Phidias.

XLIIIA. TORSO OF A LION. Life size. From Halicarnassus, Budrum. This and the bas-reliefs (No. XLIIIB) are the first
casts from the recently discovered marbles. M.B.M.*

XLIIIB. Series of bas-reliefs from the frieze of the Mausoleum of
Halicarnassus, Budrum, erected by Queen Artemisia to her

* M.B.M. signifies marble in British Museum.

husband, Mausolus, which was accounted one of the seven
wonders of the world. It was erected about 350 years B.C.
From the historical records, it is supposed to have been
constructed on a square base, supporting by colums a pyra-
midal structure, surmounted by a chariot with four horses.
The entire height was 104 feet. The friezes were enriched
with sculptures by Bryaxis, Leocharcs, Scopas, and Timo-
theus.—(Vide Newton's Halicarnassus.)   M.B.M.

XLIIIc. CARYATIS. From the Temple of Pandrosos, Erectheum.
7 ft. 4½ in. H.
The marble of this noble remain is in the British Museum.

XLIIID. A YOUTH, perhaps intended for Eros or Cupid. About 5 ft. H.
This figure, of which unhappily the head, right foot, and
arms are wanting, is an exquisite specimen of grace, and
simple truth of modelling and proportion. The original
marble is in the Elgin Room of the British Museum.

XLIV. to **XLIX.** Statues from the eastern pediment of the Parthenon, as also the heads of Hyperion's Horses, representing
Morning, and at the other end one of the horses of the Chariot
of Night.
Six of the eleven statues which were placed in this pediment are now in the British Museum, and these casts are
taken from them. The whole group was supposed to represent the miraculous birth of Minerva.
It is worthy of observation of all these marbles, which
were designed to be seen at the height of forty-four feet,
with their backs to the wall of the tympanum, that the
backs are as elaborately finished as the fronts. In fact, the
back of the Theseus is a grand study. Haydon concludes that
the accurate finish of parts which could never be seen arose
from "a principle of religious enthusiasm;" but we may also
conclude that these statues were publicly exhibited before
being placed with so many of their beauties out of sight; and
artists, at least, may rejoice at their deposition from their lofty
site, whereby so much hidden excellence has been revealed.

XLIV. THE HORSES OF HYPERION, or Morning. 4 ft. H., 6 ft. 5 in. W.
They were placed in the acute angle of the south end of the
pediment. Before them, Hyperion's head and arms were
just seen rising from the sea, and curbing the spirit of his
horses. These, by their play of line, carry the eye upward
towards the apex.

XLV. THESEUS (4 ft. H., 6 ft. W.), recumbent on a lion's skin, turned
towards the horses, is a figure, even though mutilated, giving
the noblest idea of sculptural art. He was the great Athenian
hero-king, who imitated the labours of Hercules. The attitude of the figure resembles that of Hercules on several coins.
Brönsted calls this figure Cephalus; but the preponderance of
evidence seems in favour of the original nomenclature.

XLVI. CERES AND PROSERPINE succeed the figure of Theseus. 5 ft. H. to top of shoulder, 6 ft. 4 in. w. The heads and hands are wanting, but the rest of the figures are sufficiently well preserved to exhibit the powers of Phidias in drapery. They are seated on low square seats, covered with folded carpets or cushions, and are designed to suit the ascending line of the upper cornice of the pediment.

XLVII. IRIS. 5 ft. H. to top of shoulder. The messenger to earth of the tidings of the miraculous birth, supposed to have formed the central group of the pediment. Whether it be correct or not to call this figure Iris, the evidence of motion in the figure and the drapery render it a valuable study.

XLVIII. ONE OF THE FATES, according to the British Museum Catalogue. 4 ft. 2 in. H. to top of shoulder. According to Brönsted, Fortune. Between this and Iris is the total lapse of the central composition; and this figure is under the descending line of the pediment towards the north. It is seated, simple in pose, and remarkable for the beauty of the drapery.

XLIX. TWO OF THE FATES (3 ft. 8 in. H., 7 ft. 5 in. w.), and Head of the Horse of Night. One of the Fates is recumbent, resting on the knee of her sister, who is seated. This group occupied the northern angle of the pediment.

L. ILISSUS. 2 ft. 6 in. H, 6 ft. w. A recumbent figure of a river god from the extreme north angle of the western pediment. Mr. Lloyd calls it Cephissus, and gives that of Ilissus to a corresponding figure at the southern angle of this pediment.

GRECO-ROMAN STATUES.

The restorations referred to are those in the original statues.

LI. VENUS or DIONE. Townley Collection, British Museum. 6 ft. 7 in. H. The original statue, which was found at Ostia, among the ruins of the baths of Claudius, in 1776, is in marble, in two pieces, joined, as is also the cast, at the lower part of the body, within the drapery. A similar statue, called the Venus of Arles, where it was found, is in the Louvre. The left arm, right hand, and tip of the nose are restorations.

LII. APOLLO BELVEDERE. From the Vatican. 6 ft. 11 in. H. The original statue, in marble, was found towards the close of the fifteenth century among the ruins of Antium; was purchased by a cardinal, afterwards Julius II., and subsequently placed by him in the Belvedere of the Vatican. Hence its peculiar title.

The intention of this statue has been variously read. Generally, it is supposed to represent Apollo, as son of Jupiter and Latona, destroying the children of Niobe with arrows; while it is also supposed to represent him in his medical capacity, as the Healer, after the plague at Athens; and the serpent on the stem of the tree on which his right hand rests is emblematic of health and medicine. The marble is most probably a copy from an ancient bronze, as the drapery thrown over the left arm and the general pose would seem more practicable in metal than in marble.

The entire right fore-arm and left hand were restored by Montorsolo, a pupil of Michel Angelo. Presented by Lord Cloncurry.

LIII. Discobolus or Quoit Thrower. From the Vatican. 5 ft. 10 in. h.

This statue was found at Tivoli, and is attributed to Myron, a Greek sculptor. There is a repetition in the British Museum.

The arms, right leg, and, it is said, the head, are restorations.

LIV. Mercury, called Antinous. 6 ft. 5 in. h.

This statue has been ranked with the Apollo Belvedere and Farnese Hercules as a model for artists. Poussin made it the object of constant study. It has been generally considered to represent Antinous ; but Visconti recognises it as Mercury by the curled hair, the beauty of the features, the drapery over the left arm, and the trunk of the palm tree, the leaves of which were used for writing upon.

The original, in marble of Paros, is in Rome. It was discovered in the Esquiline Mount, near the baths of Titus. No restoration was attempted ; but in replacing the legs, which were broken, the right leg was not placed properly upon the foot ; hence the obvious defect in the whole limb. Presented by Lord Cloncurry.

LV. Antinous of the Capitol—Rome. 5 ft. 11 in. h.

Found in Hadrian's Villa. It represents Antinous, the favourite of the Emperor Hadrian, who is said to have been drowned in the Nile. The right hand originally held a Caduceus.

The right leg, from the knee downward, the left foot, and fore-arm and two fingers of the right hand are restorations. Presented by Lord Cloncurry.

LVI. Meleager. From the Vatican. 6 ft. 6 in. h.

It represents the son of King Æneus, who slew the boar which was ravaging his father's country. The original statue, in grey Greek marble, was found in Rome in the sixteenth century. The left hand was wanting, and has been restored as originally holding a spear. To the right of Meleager is a dog, and on his left, placed upon a rock, a boar's head. Presented by Lord Cloncurry.

LVII. Rondinini Faun. British Museum. 5 ft. 9¾ in. h.

It is in a dancing attitude.

LVIII. Laocoon. From the Vatican. 6 ft. 3 in. h., 4 ft. 9 in. w., 7 ft. 2 in. to top of the outstretched hand.

The original of this group, in Grechetto marble, was found

in the ruins of the palace of Titus in 1506. Laocoon, who was son of Priam, and priest of Apollo, had denounced the wooden horse devised by the Greeks to introduce within its body a force into Troy, and had used his best efforts to prevent its entry; thus drawing upon himself the vengeance of the gods, who had willed the destruction of Troy. The group represents him and his two sons struggling in death agony against the serpents sent by the gods.

The right hand of the eldest son, the right arm and foot of the younger son and the right arm of Laocoon are restorations. The original group is supposed to be the work of three Rhodian sculptors—Apollodorus, Athenodorus, and Agesander, and is described by Pliny, who saw it in the palace of Titus. Another restoration is in Florence, in which the right arm of Laocoon is bent towards the head. Presented by Lord Cloncurry.

LIX. VENUS, Aphrodite, commonly designated the Crouching Venus. From the Vatican. Small life-size.

This is a modern copy in marble, executed in Rome by Vanelli, of a statue found towards the close of the last century at Salona.

The end of the right foot, the left hand, right fore-arm, the hair, and upper part of the head are restorations. Presented by Mrs. Carmichael.

LX. BOY EXTRACTING A THORN. From the Capitol. Small life-size.

Modern copy, in marble, by Vanelli, from the bronze statue. Visconti imagines it intended to represent a young Greek victor in the races of the Stadium, where boys were allowed to contend. Presented by Mrs. Carmichael.

LXI. ARIADNE. From the British Museum. 4 ft. 9 in. H.

She holds the Thyrsus in her right hand over her shoulder, a bunch of grapes in her left hand ; a young panther sports at her feet.

LXII. CUPID BENDING HIS BOW. 4 ft. 1 in. H.

Supposed to be one of the many imitations of the celebrated marble by Praxiteles. The limbs and accessories have been restored. From the collection of the Right Honourable Edmund Burke. M.B.M.

LXIII. CANEPHORA, or CARYATIS. 7 ft. 4½ in. H.

She bears a Modius on her head, which originally supported part of the entablature of a portico ; draped in a *diploidion* or double tunic, with a Peplus attached by a fibula, and richly adorned with necklaces, bracelets, and earrings. Found with four similar figures, one of which is inscribed with the names of the sculptors, Criton and Nicolaus, on the site of a supposed temple of Bacchus, near the Via Appia. M.B.M. As a contrast to the pure Grecian art in the Caryatis, xliii. c., it is useful.

LXIV. Actæon defending himself from his Dogs. 2 ft. 10 in.
H., 2 ft. 3 in. w. at base.

He wears a lion's skin over his shoulder, and with a club
upraised, seeks to strike down his dogs, Melampus and Ich-
nobates, who have seized upon his right leg. He has the
stag's horns on his head which sprung up at the command
of Diana. Found in the villa of Antoninus Pius, near Civita
Lavinia. M.B.M.

LXV. Venus. 3 ft. 4 in. H.

This graceful statue seems to have been wrongly restored,
as there is evidence of her having originally held some object in contact with her chin. Some drapery falls from her
right leg. Found at Ostia, in 1775. M.B.M.

LXVI. Victory sacrificing a Bull. 2 ft. H., 11 in. w.

LXVII. Victory sacrificing a Bull. Same size.

These two groups were found, in 1773, by Mr. Gavin Hamilton, in the ruins of the villa of Antoninus Pius, near the
ancient Lanuvium. M.B.M.

LXVIII. Nymph of Diana. 1 ft. 10 in. H., 2 ft. 3 in. w.

This figure of a draped female, less than life-size, partly
recumbent, leaning on her left hand on the ground, has the
right stretched forward and open. It is similar in action to
the figure in the Louvre, called Joueuse aux osselets ; but is
styled, in the Synopsis of British Museum, a Nymph of Diana
resting after the chase. For this reading the only apparent
reason is that she holds a bow in her left hand. Found in
1766 near the Salarian gate of Rome, in the Villa Verospi,
supposed to have been the site of the Gardens of Sallust.
M.B.M.

LXIX. Satyr, or Faun. 3 ft. 9 in. H.

He looks up, laughing; holds a set of pandean pipes in his
right hand, a club in his left, and has the skin of a fawn
thrown over his shoulders. Formerly in the Macaroni Palace
at Rome. M.B.M.

BUSTS.

LXX. Antinous. Colossal, in the character of Bacchus crowned
with ivy. This head, with several parts of the statue to
which it belonged, was found in 1770 in small pieces used
as stones in a wall, erected during the barbarous ages in
the grounds called La Tenuta della Tedesca, near the Villa
Pamphile, Rome. M.B.M.

LXXI. Hercules. A colossal head, dug up at the foot of Mount
Vesuvius, where it had been buried under the lava from that
volcano. From Sir William Hamilton's collection.—M.B.M.

LXXII. Unknown. Brought to England by Mr. Lyde Brown. It
is sometimes, but erroneously, called the German prisoner ;
there is nothing Teutonic in the countenance ; on the contrary,
it is more Celtic ; it is variously called Arminius, Decebatus.
Caractacus. Original M.B.M.

LXXIII. DIOMEDES, so called; otherwise one of the Homeric heroes. Found in 1771, by Mr. Gavin Hamilton, in that part of Hadrian's Villa called Pantinella. Nose, small portion of each lip, lobe of left ear, and bust modern restorations. M.B.M.

LXXIV. MINERVA. The head only is antique. It was found in 1784 in the Villa Casali, among ruins supposed to have belonged to the baths of Olympiodorus. The helmet and the bust, which are of bronze (in the original) are, with some variation, copied from an ancient bust of Minerva which was formerly in the Vatican; but is now in Paris.

LXXV. DIONE, the Mother of Venus. M.B.M.

LXXVI. TRAJAN, Roman Emperor. This bust is remarkable for its low forehead, which, however, is found on all coins of this Emperor. Discovered in the Campagna of Rome in 1776 by Mr. Gavin Hamilton.

LXXVII. AUGUSTUS. Formerly in the collection of Edmund Burke. M.B.M.

LXXVIII. THE BEARDED BACCHUS. A terminal head of very early Greek work. This head was found in 1790, in that part of Hadrian's Villa, Tiburtina, supposed to have been the picture gallery. M.B.M.

LXXIX. PLAUTILLA, wife of the Emperor Caracalla. M.B.M.

LXXX. EMPRESS FAUSTINA, the younger. M.B.M.

LXXXI. FEMALE HEAD. Unknown. The sockets of the eyes are hollow, and were originally filled with coloured stones or other material. M.B.M.

LXXXII. MUSE, crowned with a wreath of laurel. M.B.M.

LXXXIII. APOLLO. Brought from Rome by Lord Cawdor. M.B.M.

LXXXIV. HEAD OF A FEMALE. Unknown. She wears her hair rolled back, and a veil falls down from the back of her head on her shoulders. From recently discovered marbles at Halicarnassus; although mutilated it is of great beauty. M.B.M.

LXXXV. JUNO, crowned with a broad indented diadem. M.B.M.

LXXXVI. HOMER. A terminal head at an advanced age; of noble character. Found among the ruins of Baiæ in 1780. M.B.M.

LXXXVII. DEMOSTHENES, the great orator and statesman, born about 380 years B.C. M.B.M.

LXXXVIII. CARACALLA. The head only is antique. It was found in 1776 in the garden of the nuns at Quattro Fontani on the Esquiline Hill. M.B.M.

LXXXIX. JULIUS CÆSAR. M.B.M.

XC. NERO. Brought from Athens by Dr. Asken in 1740. M.B.M.

XCI. ATYS. Found at Rome in the Villa Palombara. M.B.M

XCII. Jupiter. Purchased by Mr. Townley at the Duke of St. Alban's sale. M.B.M.

XCIII. Bearded Bacchus. Terminal head found in 1771 at Baiæ, in a trench with a complete terminus of Bacchus. M.B.M.

XCIV. Hippocrates, the most distinguished of ancient physicians, born at Cos about 260 years B.C. Found near Albano, among the ruins of the Villa of Marcus Varro. The nose and the upper part of the left ear, also the neck and bust, are modern. M.B.M.

XCV. Clytie.

This exquisite bust rises out of the flower of the Nymphœa lotus, and is supposed to represent Clytie, said to have been turned into a sunflower. The original, one of the Townley collection, was purchased at Naples from the Laurenzano family in 1772. M.B.M.

XCVI. Severus. He wears the imperial paludamentum. The original was found in 1776 on the Palatine Hill, in the part of the palace of the Cæsars afterwards occupied by the Villa of the Magnani. M.B.M.

MISCELLANEOUS.

XCVII. A Winged Sphinx. 3 ft. h. It anciently formed part of the base of a superb candelabrum. Found by Mr. Gavin Hamilton in the ruins of the Villa of Antoninus Pius, near the ancient Lanuvium. M.B.M.

XCVIII. Vase. 3 ft. h. It has massive upright handles, is oval in form, and ornamented all round with Bacchanalian figures. Found at Monte Cagnuolo, the site of the Villa of Antoninus Pius, near the ancient Lanuvium. M.B.M.

XCIX. Vase. 2 ft. 8 in. h. Oval form with two upright handles, which spring from the necks of swans. One side of the vase is plain, the other enriched with a group of Bacchanalians. M.B.M.

C. Head of a Goat. M.B.M.

CI. Torso of a small statue of Venus. M.B.M.

CII. Triangular base of a Candelabrum. 2 ft. 8 in. h. On the sides three genii hold each a part of the armour of Mars—namely, his helmet, his shield, and his sword. Roman period. M.B.M.

CIII. Lion's Head and Leg. One of the supports of an ancient Tripod table. M.B.M.

CIV. Keystone of a Triumphal Arch, with figure of Victory. Found in the neighbourhood of Frescati, twelve miles from Rome. M.B.M.

CV. Deification of Homer, bas-relief. He is seated on a throne at the foot of Mount Parnassus. Before the poet is a group of figures offering sacrifices to him. Above are Apollo and the nine Muses; and on the summit of the hill is Jupiter, who appears to sanction the divine honours paid to Homer.

The marble original of this was found about the middle of the seventeenth century at Frattochi, the ancient Bovillæ, on the Appian Way, about ten miles from Rome; and was purchased for the British Museum, in 1819, at a cost of £1,000. M.B.M.

CVI. FEMALE BACCHANTE, bas-relief. She is clothed in thin flowing drapery, through which the forms of her body and limbs are seen. With one hand raised above her head she holds a knife, at the same time securing a portion of her drapery which is blown behind her. It is a beautiful study of drapery in motion. In her other hand she carries the hind quarter of a kid. Originally one of the bas-reliefs on a candelabrum. Believed to be by Scopas. M.B.M.

ARCHITECTURAL.

CVII. IONIC capital from the Erectheum. M.B.M.

CVIII. FRIEZE, of the Erectheum. M.B.M.

In Picture Gallery—C—South.

CIX. BUST OF ARCHBISHOP MURRAY. Marble, by John Hogan, b. in Cork, in 1800; d. in Dublin, in 1858. Presented by the Rev. Christopher Burke, P.P.

In Historical and Portrait Gallery.

CX. BUST OF RICHARD LALOR SHEIL. Marble, by C. Moore, b. in Dublin, 1790; d. in Dublin, 1863. Presented by the Right Hon. the Lord Taunton.

In Historical and Portrait Gallery.

BUST OF THOMAS MOORE. Marble, by Christopher Moore. Presented by the Earl of Charlemont.

In Historical and Portrait Gallery.

BUST OF DANIEL MACLISE, R.A. By J. Thomas. Purchased for the Gallery in London, 1874.

In Historical and Portrait Gallery.

ADDITIONAL FOR 1866.

Vide XV. B.

CXI. ATHLETE WITH THE STRIGIL, called APOXYOMENOS. 6 ft. 4 in. H.

A youth is represented using the Strigil—a scraper or flesh brush in use in the ancient baths. This statue, remarkable for its graceful sway and truthful modelling, is supposed to be the statue by Lysippus, mentioned by Pliny as having so charmed the Emperor Tiberius, that he ordered it to be removed from its place in the baths of Agrippa to his own apartments; but the Roman people insisted on its restoration to its original site. Found in an excavation at the Vicolo delle Palme (Alley of the Palms), in the Trastevere, Rome, in 1849, now in the Vatican. Sole restoration, the extremity of the right hand.

CXII. Pudicitia, or Modesty. 6 ft. 10 in. h.

This beautiful draped figure is familiar from its frequent repetition on medallions inscribed with the name Pudicitia. It has been also called a portrait of Livia, and supposed to represent a tragic muse. It was removed by Clement XIV. (Ganganelli), from the Villa Mattei to the Vatican, in 1777.

CXIII. Calliope, the Muse of Epic Poetry. 4 ft. 5 in. h.

This figure, seated with the papyrus in one hand upon her knee, and the right hand upraised as if it held the stylus or pen as in the act of thought, is supposed to represent the Muse of Epic Poetry; by some called Clio, the Muse of History. She is seated on a rock. In the Vatican.

CXIV. Venus of Milo. 6 ft. 8 in. h.

This noblest remain of ancient art was discovered near the Theatre in the Island of Milo—the ancient Melos in 1820. For majesty and simple sway, as well as beauty of form, it is unrivalled. Many theories are raised as to the original intention of the figure, but the most probable is that derivable from the assimilation of its action to that of Venus Victrix, as seen on ancient coins, holding a polished shield in which she contemplates herself. Such is also the action of a beautiful bronze statue of a latter date, found in some ancient ruins at Brescia. The left foot is a restoration; but fortunately no further effort at restoration has been made. M. Clarac conjectures from a fragment discovered at the same time, that she held an apple in one hand, which would have been more like Venus triumphant after the decision of Paris. By some this Venus of Milo has been supposed to represent Victory. In the Louvre.

CXV. Apollo Sauroctonos, or the Lizard killer. 5 ft. 2 in. h., 1 ft. 11 in. w.

A youth is here represented resting against the stem of a tree, on which a lizard is seen, which he watches to seize. Original in Parian marble; formerly in the Villa Borghese; now in the Louvre. The entire right arm from above the wrist is a restoration.

CXVI. Diana of Gabii. 5 ft. 4 in. h.

The goddess is in the act of robing, adjusting her mantle. A statue similar in action is in the Villa Pamphili, at Rome. The marble was discovered among the ruins of the ancient Gabii; was placed in the Villa Borghese, in Rome; is now in the Louvre. The restorations are, the nose, the right hand, left sleeve, and portion of the elbow, the right foot, and half the left leg.

CXVII. Germanicus, or Mercury. 5 ft. 11 in. h.

The motive for assuming this to be the statue of Germanicus is not very clear. It is evidently the portrait of some distinguished person to whom the attributes of Mercury, at least one of them, the tortoise, are given—the chlamys falling from the left shoulder, and the left hand as if holding a caduceus, while the right is upraised as in the act of oration, are likewise similar to other statues of Mercury. An inscription on the back of the tortoise in Greek character, as follows :—"Cleomenes, son of Cleomenes, of Athens, made this." Sextus Quintus placed the statue in his villa on the Esquiline. From the Villa Negroni at Rome ; placed by Louis XIV. at Versailles ; now in the Louvre. The finger and thumb of the left hand are the only restorations.

CXVIII. Genius of Repose or Death. 5 ft. 10 in. h.

A youth with arms bent over his head, and with legs crossed, leans against the stem of a tree. Sleep and Death, regarded by us as type one of the other, were evidently so regarded by the ancients, and were similarly represented. Such seems the intention of this figure, even though the eyes are not closed. Formerly in Cardinal Mazarin's collection, now in the Louvre. Much restored, but all the pieces antique.

CXIX. Jason. 5 ft. h., 3 ft. w.

A young man is represented in the act of tying on his sandal on the right foot, raised on a block ; his left foot yet unsandaled ; his head upraised as if suddenly surprised, or gazing fixedly on some object. From the accordance of the action of this statue with the fable of Jason, it is supposed to represent the young husbandman when summoned hurriedly to the presence of Pelias to assist at a sacrifice. An oracle had previously warned Pelias, the usurper of the throne of Iolchos, the birth-right of his nephew 'Jason, to beware of a man with one sandal. Nevertheless, relying upon his own power, and anxious to see his nephew, he sent for him ; according to other accounts Jason went under the influence of an oracle. Jason arrived with the one sandal of ill omen, and subsequently slew the usurper. This statue was also considered to represent Cincinnatus. Formerly in the Villa Negroni ; purchased by Louis XIV. for Versailles ; now in the Louvre. The entire left arm, the right hand, and part of the arm are restorations. The head, although antique, is of different marble from the rest of the figure. The restorations are far inferior to the original type.

CXX. The Gladiator, or Warrior of Agasias. 5 ft. h., 3 ft. 9 in. w.

This noble statue which was found during the pontificate of Paul V., at Antium, on the sea-shore, where the Apollo (Belvedere) had been found a century previous, has generally been called the fighting Gladiator, or Borghese Gladiator, from its localization in the Villa Borghese. It is objected to the assumption of Gladiatorial title, that no known statue of a Gladiator is quite naked, yet the dying Gladiator is so. The action, however, is more that of a combatant on foot against a horseman, than one in equal combat on foot. In the Louvre. The entire right arm and right ear are restorations.

x

CXXI. Group from St. Ildefonso. 4 ft. 11 in. h., 3 ft. 4 in. w.

Many readings are given of this group, which was originally found in the Villa Ludovisi ; then with the Odesalch collection, which belonged to Queen Christina of Sweden, was brought into Spain, and first placed in the Castle of San Ildefonso. Two youths crowned with laurel and oak wreaths in graceful attitude, stand side by side ; one resting his arm on the shoulder of the other ; they both look down upon a small altar, on which one, with a cup or sacrificial cake in his hand, seems to have poured a libation, or placed a cake, and the other applies an inverted torch, while he carries a second torch upon his shoulder. Near the youth with the torches is a diminutive statue of a priestess or goddess, perhaps to indicate the goddess at whose shrine the sacrifice is made. By some the group is called Antinous and Adrian ; by others Sleep and Death. The inverted torch being generally emblematic of the latter. Now in Madrid.

CXXII. Polymnia. 6 ft. 2 in. h., 2 ft. 10 in. deep at base.

A closely draped figure with wreath of flowers on her head, leaning in contemplation on a mass of rock. Formerly in the Borghese collection at Rome, now in the Louvre. Much restoration, well executed by Penna, a Roman sculptor.

CXXIII. Hygieia. 4 ft. 7 in. h.

A young nymph closely draped holds a serpent in her right hand, which she turns towards a cup held in her left. Representation of the healing art. In the Louvre.

CXXIV. Achilles. 6 ft. 11 in. h.

This statue of the Hero of Greece has a helmet on the head, and an anclet or ring above the right ankle. Formerly in the Borghese collection, now in the Louvre. Restorations, the left fore arm, the fingers of the right hand, and tips of some of the toes.

CXXV. Roman Matron, called also Pudicitia. 7 ft. 6 in. h.

Colossal statue of a female closely enveloped in drapery, beautifully arranged and modelled ; the sway of the figure is graceful and the pose noble. It was found by Prince Elbeuf, early in the eighteenth century, in Herculaneum, and is supposed to represent one of the family of Balbus. He sent this and two similarly draped statues to Prince Eugene, at whose death they were purchased for the King of Poland for 6,000 dollars—£900, and have since remained in Dresden. Only restoration, a portion of the falling drapery on the left side.

CXXVI. Psyche—a torso. 2 ft. 10 in. h.

This beautiful remain seems to have formed part of a monument or group of some kind. From Naples.

www.ingramcontent.com/pod-product-compliance
Lightning Source LLC
Chambersburg PA
CBHW030606270326
41927CB00007B/1061